Write Dance

In the Nursery

Write Dance

In the Nursery

A pre-writing programme for children aged 3 to 5

Ragnhild A. Oussoren

P·C·P
Paul Chapman
Publishing

Paul Chapman Publishing
A SAGE Publications Company
1 Oliver's Yard
55 City Road
London EC1Y 1SP

SAGE Publications Inc.
2455 Teller Road
Thousand Oaks, California 91320

SAGE Publications India Pvt Ltd.
B-42, Panchsheel Enclave
Post Box 4109
New Delhi 110 017

Commissioning Editors: George Robinson and Barbara Maines
Editorial Team: Mel Maines, Sarah Lynch, Wendy Ogden, Mike Gibbs
Designer: Helen Weller
Illustrator: Ragnhild A. Oussoren
Translator: Rosemary Mitchell-Schuitevoerder

A catalogue record for this book is available from the British Library

Library of Congress Control Number 2005932395

ISBN 1 4129 1904 5

Printed on paper from sustainable resources

Printed in Great Britain by The Cromwell Press Ltd, Trowbridge, Wiltshire.

Dedication

For my own two little toddlers Oliver Robert and

Barnaby Charles who teach me how to be Bestemor (grandma)

Contents

Foreword

Any parent or teacher working with very young children will notice that they soon reach out for simple items such as pencils, pens and paper. They can dance to music and will do so in their own creative manner.

There is very little available on the education market for little children, because many activities and books are only designed for the slightly older infant.

In some countries children go to school at the age of two and a half, which is why we need a horizontal and vertical coherence to support all infants in the best way possible. Consequently more and more infant school teachers have tried to adapt Write Dance Part 1 to suit nursery school children.

After our experiences with the younger children in mainstream Primary Education and the recurrent request at Professional Development Courses we thought it would be a good idea to develop a pre-school Write Dance, with new songs, drawings and especially ideas with regard to psychomotor skills, working with materials and other methods. Ragnhild thought it was a great idea and we decided to find our way together towards creating a Write Dance for pre-school children. Our first trial sessions were a great success and the children loved it.

We hope you enjoy *Write Dance in the Nursery* and allow them to scrimble as much as they like!

Jocelyne Pynaert, infant school teacher with a PDC in Flanders, Belgium.

Marijke Ceunen, dance teacher with a PDC in Flanders, Belgium.

Note from the publisher:

The translation of the original book published in the Netherlands was presented in the spoken style of Ragnhild Oussoren's workshops. We have not attempted to change this in order not to lose the creative and spontaneous aspect of her work.

The Story of a Piece of Paper

Once upon a time there was a piece of paper.

'I am so lonely,' said the piece of paper, 'and I look so white, why won't anybody come and play with me?' The piece of paper was lying on the kitchen table and was very bored. Then Yoyo came into the kitchen to have a drink of squash and the piece of paper began to call Yoyo softly.

'Yoyo, come here, look I am a piece of paper!'

Yoyo didn't hear and so the piece of paper began to call a little louder.

'Yoyo, come HERE!' it shouted. 'Look, I am a piece of paper!' but Yoyo still didn't hear. Next Meema came into the kitchen to have a drink of squash and when the door opened the piece of paper fell on the floor. The piece of paper continued to call out.

'Yoyo, come here, I am a piece of paper!

This time Meema did hear it and she said to Yoyo, 'Did you hear that Yoyo? I think the piece of paper is calling you.'

Yoyo and Meema knelt down and put their ears close to the piece of paper. They both clearly heard what the piece of paper was saying.

'Thank you, oh thank you so much, would you mind colouring me, I am so white and naked.'

Yoyo and Meema quickly went to fetch their box of crayons and began to scrimble all kinds of things on the piece of paper.

They now heard the piece of paper starting to giggle and laugh because the colouring and squiggling of the crayons and pencils tickled. Yoyo and Meema turned it into a real piece of art.

Finally Meema said, 'Dear little piece of paper, are you happy now?'

'Yes, thank you, oh thank you so much, now make me fly quickly! Yoyo folded the paper into a wonderful plane and sent it flying through the room.

'Oops!' They heard the paper say. 'It tickles in my tummy', and crash… it tumbled into the plants.

'Once more Yoyo, I want to fly again,' called the piece of paper from the plant box.

Well, Yoyo and Meema continued to play for hours and hours with the piece of paper they had coloured themselves. It landed under the table and on top of the cupboard, on the counter with its tip near the jam jar ('Wow, delicious!' they heard it say), on the stove, next to the cat litter and last of all… in the sink with a little bit of water at the bottom.

'Oh dear, oh no, now I can no longer fly,' said the piece of paper sadly, but Yoyo lifted it out carefully, and put it down on the windowsill and spoke gently.

'Don't worry, dear little pretty coloured piece of paper, tomorrow your wings will have dried again and we will play with you. Go to sleep now, it is dark. Sleep well…' and Yoyo and Meema closed the door of the kitchen quietly.

What about the piece of paper? It fell asleep straightaway; it was exhausted after all that flying!

How the Audio CD is Arranged

The audio CD is arranged as follows:

Home Stories	Page	CD track no. solo	CD track no. instruments
H1 Sandy Hill	19	1	2
H2 Kringeli-krangeli	25	3	4
H3 Pat-a-cake	31	5	6
H4 The Staircase	37	7	8
H5 The Toy Train	43	9	10
H6 Tickle Tree	49	11	12
H7 Little Water Shute	53	13	14
H8 The Rainbow	59	15	16
H9 Little Sun	65	17	18
H10 Straight, Bent, Cross, Happy	71	S 19	S 20
	71	B 21	B 22
	71	C 23	C 24
	71	H 25	H 26

Funfair Stories	Page	CD track no. solo	CD track no. instruments
F1 Watermill	77	27	28
F2 My Dinky Car	81	29	30
F3 Merry-go-round	85	31	32
F4 Procession	89	33	34
F5 Air Train	93	35	36
F6 Tree & Fairy Lights	97	37	38
F7 Big Water Shute	101	39	40
F8 The Gateway	105	41	42
F9 Dear Sun, Dear Moon	109	43	44

Introduction

What is Write Dance?

Write Dance is a handwriting methodology and handwriting method designed for all children in primary education, including children with physical or mental disabilities. Write Dance tries to teach children to write starting from their own emotions and natural movements, giving it their own 'swing'. Creating movements from their own emotions is of prime importance. A good shape, a 'beautiful' letter, cannot be created until the basic movement is smooth, flowing and performed with enough self-confidence. For example, Write Dance encourages children to feel what a

letter 'o' is like, hear it and experience it before they actually begin to write it. That is why we practise the movements live and in our spaces. Only then do we scrimble, 'write draw' and write on board, paper or any other writing surface. Writing movements made to sounds, noises and music help the 'o' to become and remain rounded, so that the children will eventually know how to make it smaller, without having to will themselves or feeling pushed, in other words without forcing the shape or pressing too hard on their writing utensils. Only then can they write a beautifully rounded and healthy 'o' and the 'o' will become their personal 'o'.

Write Dance and music, songs, rhymes and games are inseparable. The basic movements are automated and programmed playfully and stored in the motor centre in the brain so that initial writing can be performed without forced effort and frustration and can provide on-going pleasure. All the actions are concentrated on making the children feel happy and comfortable with their bodies. They cannot make mistakes, any expression is a good expression, even if the paper is torn up, crumpled up or thrown away angrily. And that isn't wrong either, because all the child is doing is getting rid of her frustrations! Write Dance offers plenty of opportunities for movements to come naturally, drawing upon emotional experiences and linking to their own fantasy world, which is the best way to encourage learning to write. Write Dance focuses on the child, and their inner experiences will continue to be the prime guideline.

Pre-school Write Dance

The unique features of Write Dance; its child centredness, its appeal to emotions that are immediately expressed in

movements without the need to achieve or perform, make it ideally suited to start with children at a very early age. That is why this publication of *Write Dance in the Nursery* should be seen as a complete re-draft of *Write Dance Part 1* (written for four to eight year olds) adjusted entirely to the pre-school age group. *Write Dance in the Nursery* contains nine themes, each one with a 'Home' and a 'Funfair' alternative. Certain basic movements will be central to each theme, and will continue to be developed in two ways, once in Home and once in Funfair. You will find a more comprehensive summary in the tables at the beginning of this book. There is a song on the CD for both Home and Funfair alternatives. All the songs have been composed specifically for pre-school Write Dance. There is also an instrumental, unsung version on the CD. In this programme there is always an introductory story and the lyrics of the song, including suggestions for 'Movements in Your Spaces' and 'Scrimbling'. The movements and expressions on the writing surface are explained in detail for the first verse under the heading Scrimbling, while the second (and possibly third) verse will only offer a few new sentences with 'scrimble' suggestions. There is always a section called 'Theme Play' with ideas for games and how to work with sensory materials.

Movements in your space

Most movements can be performed standing, walking, sitting or even lying down. Usually there will also be an alternative available for 'walking movements' which allows the children to sit. The teacher will not find  the simple lyrics and tunes of the songs and accompanying descriptions of movements in their spaces difficult. Initially the movements will feel a bit strange to some of the children, which does not matter. Firstly it is important to initiate general movements by listening, seeing, imitating, experiencing and doing them. We may leave out playing the music initially and practise the basic movements (such as walking straight or bent, turning wrists or hands), each accompanied by our own noises, sounds or words several times in succession. Children who do not want to join in at all are allowed to watch, lie on the floor, 'thrash about' or move in their own time. Generally a child will join in after a while of their own accord. It is no use forcing them. This has never been the intention of write dancing. Moving with their entire bodies is always a good preparation for scrimbling or writing movements on self-made boards, paper or any other writing surfaces. While moving on their writing surface it is not at all surprising to see movements evolve spontaneously into arms going up in the air, or standing up, walking or dancing.

Movements on a writing surface

'Scrimbling' is a coined word for Write Dance and means working on a writing surface by:

- scribbling
- wriggling
- doodling
- circling
- experiencing and experimenting.

The children will scrimble with a scrimbling instrument on a scrimbling surface, where both instrument and surface should be taken in the broadest sense. For instance, 'finger dancing' is scrimbling with your fingers, straight on the table top or on the board, first on their own bodies and then, for example, on somebody else's back. Finger dancing over the 'scrimbles', which have just been completed in chalk will encourage recognition and can be a practical way of starting revision. The German word 'Fingerspitzengefühl', meaning the intuitive feeling at your finger tips, refers to the signals that are being sent to the big programme in your brain. We like to offer the children a great variety of scrimbling tools and scrimbling surfaces.

Important! Under the heading 'scrimbling' we sometimes offer two suggestions. The second suggestion is for pre-school children and infants who have already done some early scrimbling a number of times, have heard the song many times and are ready for some variations. The teacher will notice immediately when a child is ready for such variations. It is best to sing one or two lines first, without music, so that the children can indicate their own pace and skill.

Both hands

Just like we did in 'write drawing' in the original book, *Write Dance*, we will 'scrimble' as much as possible with both hands. This comes naturally to pre-school children and it stimulates the two halves of our brain. The left and right hemispheres have different functions which we will need all our lives. Although left or right-handedness develops after the second year, which is known as 'lateralisation', we should still give pre-school children's hands equal chances. Moving around in their spaces will make it very easy and we will immediately notice if there are any problems and where there might be psychomotor issues in the future.

Consolidating

Basic movements on the writing surface may be expressed slowly or quickly, big or small, with strong or gentle pressure, round or straight and so on, which we will always do with as many colours as possible. The repetition of movement in different colours over each other is called 'consolidating' in typical Write Dance terminology. We could compare it with a river that has been running down the rocks for years, streaming or thundering and cutting out a shape. In the same way scrimbling will create personal shapes (letters eventually) by means of 'the personal swing' a child attaches to her movements. This personal 'swing' is established by repeatedly practising hand-eye co-ordination: a child will perceive with her eyes what is happening on the writing surface, feel and experience it with her hand(s) and hear the accompanying sounds, noises and music. Consolidating in child language means: doing and repeating the movements over each other, with their own swing and the momentum of successive moments – in other words: NO tracing!

Experiencing and emotions

Writing is intrinsically related to emotions. This link is maybe most apparent when the emotions are blocked. The shapes of the letters cannot be created smoothly and in a flowing style. They will have 'frozen', which becomes apparent when we see the children pressing too hard on their writing utensils, and consequently producing impulsive unintentional strokes, closed letters, words and sentences too close to each other and the abrupt breaking off of letters. However, if the emotions can be freed, the rest will follow and most of all self-confidence will return. This self-confidence is an inexhaustible source for creativity, games and social and motor skills, but also for managing cognitive subject material. Even though scrimbling doesn't initially need to 'mesh' with the music, movements converted into a play of colours will already provide a print of the young child's perception of their environment. The song drawings will represent real creations: expression or reflection of their personality in constant development. The more variation children can use to express themselves in basic movements, for example cheerfully and cross, intensively and carefully, firm and relaxed, ugly and pretty, mad and normally, the more they will be able to move more freely on a smaller writing surface.

Repetition and routine

The repetition of movements, routines and rituals, telling the same stories or fairy-tales, singing the same songs will give a young child, including a child with developmental problems, a sense of trust and safety in which lies the core and strength of the repetition process. Repetitions are rudimental needs leading to development across a wide area. Consider sowing and harvesting a cornfield or a field full of flowers. If you know the words, songs, dance steps, scales and exercises by heart, the moment has arrived for you to make variations and to let your imagination loose. The physical, sound or artistic movements will be performed in a range of variations. 'Being different' or 'being silly' may have positive results, allowing the child to acquire a strong sense of contrasting emotions or expressions. It is fun to scrimble on the board, but even more so with your feet and your nose. The revision activities we choose to perform need to remain challenging and should fit in with the child's world of movements. Therefore we will always perform the basic movements in our spaces in the same way, but each time it will be a new situation, a new day, a new week in another season and thus offering us new experiences. We will always give the child enough time to say what they feel and experience, both in their bodies and in their perceptions on the writing surface.

Development

Once the child has got used to scrimbling, it could become a daily recurrent activity available whenever they feel like it and feel safe and secure using the writing surface.

The older the child, the more they will be able to control their movements in their spaces and on their writing surfaces. They will feel they have mastered their 'controls' and that is when the teacher or parent/carer of today should step back from encouraging the child to produce beautiful, resembling or 'perfect' shapes. As we, in our society, remain focused on hitting targets, the reduction of input, diligence and ambition with its related muscular efforts might appear odd at first. Heavy pressure on a pencil produces a deeper colour which 'proves' you can produce a shape. Once again, the opposite, that is, applying less pressure and repeating the movements over each other, has a healing effect in our lives today.

In our technical age, contrary to what we are used to in education, we should be striving to achieving perfect shapes.

The Scrimbling area

Preferably this should be a permanent area with a self-made board attached to the wall with one or two separate boards within reach ready to 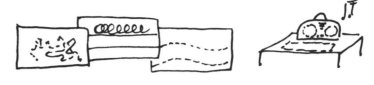 be put on the table. It is possible to paint a table with blackboard paint, which can be used as a Write Dance table. A tray with pieces of chalk and a tray with small pieces of sponge should be included. In addition there should be rolls of wallpaper, large sheets of paper, pieces of chalk and possibly other materials, for example, a tray with bird sand (available from a pet shop). Of course a CD-player will be needed.

Materials for the writing surface

Boards

Use sheets of MDF cut to size, (for example, 1022 x 600mm) so that the children can work side by side or opposite each other, or half the size, suitable for one child. The thickness could be 4 or 6mm. Paint both sides with blackboard paint (any colour). Usually it is sufficient to pass over it once or twice with a roller of paint on front and back. It is also possible to paint lines or waves for a special effect on some boards. The boards can be held in place with non-slip mats, but that might not be necessary. Blu-Tac could help stick them down to the table, too.

Write Dance table

This is an ordinary rectangular or round (old) table painted with blackboard paint and it is always available for the child to scrimble on. The legs of the table are cut off at child height. A hole can be cut out with a diameter of about 450 mm in the centre of the round table, big enough for one child to stand in where they can scrimble around themselves. If you stand in the middle you will be the centre of attention and play an important part. It also helps the child to find their bearings in a circle.

Tip: You might be able to buy an old coffee table in a second hand shop for very little money. These tables are just the right height. Paint them with blackboard paint and your Write Dance table is ready to use.

Scrimbling den (hinged board)

Make this from two standard MDF-sheets (122 x 600mm) and 8mm thick. Paint the boards with blackboard paint in the required colour(s) and have two semi-circles cut out with diameters of 30mm. Fix three strong hinges to the longer sides. The boards are set on the ground in an A-shape and a child can sit on either side with legs stuck through the semi-circle. The intention of this exercise is to experience arches in, for example, the Rainbow and Gateway themes, using pieces of chalk, sponges and simply by finger dancing, using wet or dry materials. To prevent the boards from closing attach an aluminium strip of approximately 3 x 4mm wide in the correct position. Drill a hole and secure it with a screw and two eyes. On the opposite side you need to file away a semi-circle so that this opening fits exactly round the screw on the other side. This is done on both sides so that this 'scrimbling den' can also be considered safe for other purposes.

Paper

All types and sizes are suitable. Ask a printer for leftovers because Write Dance needs a lot of paper. Slippy paper is unsuitable. Rolls of wallpaper without relief or large sheets of drawing or painting paper can be used too. We always Write Dance on large surfaces. If you don't have any of these at hand but you do have some plain A4 paper you can always draw or reinforce the movements on top of each other with colour crayons or pieces of chalk. After all, it is all about movement and not about producing a lovely perfect shape or figure.

Sticky materials or masking tape

As both hands will be used attach the sheets of paper with sticky materials, for example, Blu-Tac, masking tape or plasticine. Plain sticky tape is not really suitable because it is difficult to remove from the tables afterwards.

A large sheet of plastic

This is perfect for doodling or scrimbling. A large piece of plastic can also be filled with a little water, provided it is held by some children and their teacher. Put a little bit of crepe paper in it and the water will colour while swaying it gently from side to side. If you add some bath foam, some paint and little balls or marbles, it will give you a wonderful display of colour.

Writing materials

Chalk

Plain blackboard chalk is suitable, but do consider asthmatic children who react to chalk dust. Use as many colours as possible.

Old or short wax crayons

These are always suitable, while new and long pieces of crayon might break while using them, which could lead to unnecessary disappointment. Moreover old pieces of crayon can be gripped from the top, which is conducive to preparing the hand position for when they are ready to do some real handwriting.

Chunky short markers

These are always popular with any child as the colours are bright, but wax crayons are more durable and it is the movements that count and not the results. It is always advisable to vary materials.

Plain pencils

These are not quite as suitable to be held in both hands as pre-school children can't grip them well in their little fists (not even if they are thick pencils). However, if they use one pencil only as a temporary alternative it is possible for them to copy the basic movements on top of each other, or to reinforce them.

Sponges

Cut a standard cleaning sponge into six to eight small pieces and place them in small trays with a little water. Dry cloths should always be available. Children who are not yet capable of holding pieces of chalk enjoy playing on the board with sponges. Squeezing sponges, drying the surface (with the basic movements) and wiping and stamping their feet all make perception and experiences enjoyable, regardless of the level of development of their motor skills.

Tip: Attach pegs to the sponges if it is not desirable to have wet hands. It is also possible to use little sticks (100 x 120mm), wrapped in a piece of foam plastic, secured with fine wire for paint scrimbling.

Scrimbling and Write Dancing with sponges is an option too!

Rubber gloves

These are handy and easy for practising dry or wet movements on the surface, and movements with shaving or bath foam.

Chunky brushes

The focus of the movements should be on coarse motor skills. First allow the children to scrimble with their hands, next with their fingers, their fingertips and then, for example, with chunky brushes.

Cotton wool and cotton wool balls

These make a nice soft material to rub over your body or, if they are a little damp, to make prints on the table and on the board or on a plastic surface. Messing and squeezing while playing with water can be turned into fun games.

Shaving foam

This makes a perfect Write Dance material. It smells great and they can squiggle around in it, draw lines and dots, or anything you can imagine. Use a dropping pipette to introduce a water colour which makes wonderful effects. Keep it slippery with some bath foam or fill an empty shower spray with water and spray it over the bath foam now and again.

Bath foam

This can also be used for writing movements or scrimbling, or even to wash teddies (see Theme Play in Little Water Shute).

Finger paint

This makes a wonderful slippery material if it is mixed with wallpaper paste, salad oil or a lubricant. We can make some prints by laying a sheet of drawing paper over it and sliding our hands over the top to bring out the print as if by magic.

Finger dancing

This is something which we will only do with our fingers on the table top if there isn't any writing material readily available. If we can feel what it is like to work with dry and wet materials on the self-made board, then the feet can serve, too, which makes it very exciting.

Paper eye masks

Scrimbling with their eyes shut or wearing a mask stimulates sensory perception, sense of touch and free movement. Only do it if the child is ready for it. Many pre-school children might feel frightened when they can't see, while others might consider it a challenge. The surprise when they take off their masks and see what they have created on the writing surface always gives them a lot of pleasure and encourages their self-confidence. Playing with 'warm water masks' on their bodies or on their faces will have a similar effect.

Materials for theme play

Movements in their spaces:

- ribbons, scarves, streamers, garlands, strips of material, strips of paper or newspaper, polystyrene, confetti

- soft materials need to be put on a sheet, which can be held by a couple of children

- a big sheet of plastic to scrimble on or to put some water in with a piece of crepe paper.

On the floor:

- skittles, boxes, hoops, tracks drawn in chalk, ropes, and strips or snippets of paper or cloth.

The Role of the teacher

Moving

The role of the adult is to offer the opportunity to make as many movements as possible, to offer enough space and material for experiments and to discover new things. It will be necessary to establish a certain routine before it is possible to think up variations together with the children. A routine opens up ways to free fantasies and fun, in their spaces, on their boards as well as on paper.

Reading out and telling stories

Once a new theme is due, it is obvious that you need to begin with reading the story. The child will soon discover the freedom to add their own experiences, which encourages the powers of their imagination and creativity. It is possible to present the stories and songs in succession according to the alternatives within 'Home' and 'Funfair', but it is also possible to combine and alternate, depending on special days, events, holidays or seasons.

Sitting and standing

In order to keep the transition from the well-known reading of a familiar story to unfamiliar 'movements' low key, the teacher should begin with demonstrating the movements sitting down without any music but with appropriate sounds or noises after having read the story and listening to all the tales. The children will then copy the movements while seated. Next the movements can be repeated while standing. The children will be eager to join in of their own accord. Moving their bodies comes naturally to all children.

Should I join in?

If one child refuses to join for a considerable time, it might be because they are already demonstrating coarse motor skill problems and they need to be observed. It means that a good interaction between their emotions and physical performance is lacking. Such a child has frozen and might need special help and assistance to begin to move naturally again.

Scrimbling

The teacher will need to demonstrate and join in during the transition from moving in their spaces to scrimbling. Adults need to watch that there is a balance between scrimbling (or repeated movements) and plain drawing. Children learn from their parents or older siblings how they can draw dolls, figures, shapes and letters. They will proudly want to show their teacher what they can do. It has been like that since the introduction of compulsory education. However, in our age of technology with insufficient links between coarse and fine motor skill movements, experiences and emotions, pre-school Write Dance and its invaluable scrimbling can be a means to preparing a pre-school child's sensomotor and psychomotor skills for infant activities.

Write Dance

We hope that *Write Dance in the Nursery* will be continued and possibly combined with Write Dance, so that when children begin to learn to write letters and join ups, they are completely ready. Moreover, we would like them to enjoy what they do and produce smooth, flowing and springy first sentences and a flow of words on paper. When pre-school children or infants begin to make their own combinations of movements and Write Dance in their own games and drawings, we can assume that the preparatory writing signs have been well stored in their brain programme. The teacher does not need to force or impose anything. It would only have a contrary effect and Write Dancing would overshoot its goal.

Pieces of chalk

It is not unusual for a pre-school child to take hold of pieces of chalk initially in a hammer grip. It means that the wrists are vertical and the fingers are gripping the pieces of chalk like you would grip a hammer. Hand and wrist exercises in their spaces, finger dancing on the table, scrimbling in shaving cream and bath foam and finger paint will loosen up the child's little wrists meaning they will also be able to grip the pieces of chalk from the top, which is beneficial to writing at a later stage. Gripping the chalk from the top causes the wrists to twist inward which in turn encourages the brain stimuli and enables development, for example, having a better view of the writing surface, applying variations and adding drawings. It is right to offer some corrections now and then to do scrimbling on paper, though without force.

The board

If a child does not respond, or if they find it annoying because their wrists are still too stiff, the board and the accompanying sponges and cloths are a suitable means to work with wet and dry materials. Pressing down on pieces of chalk when they get wet, makes a lovely mess and could be continued in shaving foam, bath foam, water, sand and wet clay. All this helps to loosen up the wrists.

Tip: Any paper Write Dance works of art made by the children, which they don't wish to take with them and they have parted with, can be folded by the teacher and cut into a shape such as a butterfly, a heart, an apple. Thus the child sees that a shape is hidden in their actions. They could also be used as a background for handicrafts and three-dimensional art works.

Stars in the text

Some suggestions for 'theme play' will be marked with a star, as well as some movements and scrimbles.

It means that such an assignment is still too difficult for the youngest children.

Illustrations

The illustrations are very simple which makes them easy to copy and they can be used as a source of inspiration. If necessary they can be enlarged, coloured and pasted onto something so that the children can scrimble around them.

H6

H5

H7

Similarities in basic movements and sensory experiences

Home	Funfair	How to experience basic writing movements on a writing surface in a sensory way
1. Sandy Hill	Watermill	Straight 'ship' or rocking movements – upwards and downwards or swaying. *Experience wet or dry play with sand and water.*
2. Kringeli-krangeli	My Dinky Car	Swinging movements and lines. *Finding or losing their way, or finding their bearings and making their way home.*
3. Pat-a-cake	Merry-go-round	Circular movements, continuous tune. *Fat, full, bloated, dizzy.*
4. The Staircase	Procession	Angular movements, rhythm and counting. *High, low, in a line and regularity.*
5. The Toy Train	Air Train	Looped movements upwards and downwards, quickly and slowly. *Quickly and slowly, down on the floor and up above.*
6. Tickle Tree	Tree & Fairy Lights	Random and focused (grabbing) movements. *Set to the ground and freely in their spaces.*
7. Little Water Shute	Big Water Shute	Swaying movements. *Water, agility, calm or rough, high and low.*
8. The Rainbow	The Gateway	Arched movements. *Arches, standing up, safety and protection.*
9. Little Sun	Dear Sun, Dear Moon	Circular and straight movements starting from a fixed or central point. *Heat and cold, summer and winter, nearby and far away, 'me and you'.*
10. Straight, Bent, Cross, Happy		Straight and circular, set and free movements. *Set ways, flexibility, adjustment, feelings and emotions.*

The connection between the themes in Write Dance in the Nursery and Write Dance

Write Dance in the Nursery Scrimbling Song drawings Home and Funfair		Write Dance Write drawings Music drawings Nine weekly themes	
1. Sandy Hill	Watermill	1. Volcano	
2. Kringeli-krangeli	My Dinky Car	2. Countryside Walk and Krongelidong Animals	
3. Pat-a-cake	Merry-go-round	3. Circles and Eights	
4. The Staircase	The Procession	4. Robot	
5. The Toy Train	Air Train	5. Train	
6. Tickle Tree	Tree & Fairy Lights	6. Tree	
7. Little Water Shute	Big Water Shute	7. Silver Wings	
8. The Rainbow	The Gateway	8. Cats	
9. Little Sun	Dear Sun, Dear Moon	9. Mandala	
10. Straight, Bent, Cross, Happy		No matching theme	

A working method in Ten Steps for Write Dance in the Nursery

1. Stick down sensory or scrimble materials beforehand and fasten down the paper with Blu-Tac or masking tape. Provide sufficient wet sponges and dry cloths.

2. Read out the story several times.

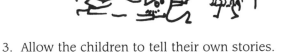

3. Allow the children to tell their own stories.

4. Demonstrates movements with sounds and noises.

5. Ask the children to copy them.

6. Sing accompanied or unaccompanied by the CD.

7. Perform actions accompanied by music.

8. Continue actions accompanied by instrumental music.

9. Scrimbling and/or working with sensory materials or playing games and repeating songs with actions.

10. Repeat scrimbling.

This working method develops gradually and some points are repeated several times before progressing to the next point. Allow plenty of time, days if necessary. After all, very young children can only keep their attention to an assignment for 15 to 20 minutes and repetition creates confidence, pleasure and safety.

Stories, Movements, Theme Plays and Scrimbling

Home Stories

H1

Sandy Hill

Matching Theme Funfair:
Watermill

Yoyo and Meema are going to the beach with their Mum. They both have their buckets and spades. Meema has a red spade and a blue bucket, Yoyo has a green spade and a yellow bucket.

'Look, there's the sea,' says Meema. 'Are you going in with me, Yoyo?'

They both run into the water. Crash! Yoyo trips and is soaking wet. Meema and Mum have to laugh. 'Fortunately you were wearing your swimming trunks,' said Mum. Quickly Yoyo takes off his t-shirt and trousers and begins to roll in the waves.

'Don't go any further, Yoyo,' says Mum. But of course Yoyo already knows.

'Come on, Yoyo, we will make a high sand hill,' says Meema and starts digging with her red spade. Yoyo gets out of the water and picks up his green spade.

'I will make my hill here,' he says. It is a warm day, so Yoyo dries quickly.

'Your hill is much bigger than mine, Yoyo,' says Meema, 'will you come and help me?' Yoyo, a strong boy, immediately throws a big spade full of sand on Meema's hill. Then they fill Yoyo's buckets of water and they use Mum's hairbrush to make rain over their sand hills. They dip the brush in water and give it a good shake.

'Now it is raining heavily,' says Meema. She has found another brush in her beachbag and beats both brushes creating big drops on her sand hill. They press down the sand of their hills with their feet and begin to dig burrows.

'Wobble, wobble, wobble,' says Meema and Yoyo joins in. And then she suddenly discovers she has covered her little blue bucket with sand.

On the beach – lots of sa-and,
On the beach – lots of sa-and.
My hill is here, your hill is there.
They make a fine pair.

2nd verse

My hill is high, so very hi-igh,
Your hill is high, so very hi-igh.
I'm tumbling down, look here,
Wobble, wobble, wobble…
Oh dear.

3rd verse

Here comes a cloud, a big big clou-oud,
Here comes a cloud, a big big clou-oud.
It's raining on my hill,
Tippy, tappy, tat,
I'm wet.

H1

Movements

Words	Movements
On the beach - lots of sa-and, On the beach - lots of sa-and.	Digging movements from side to side: dig down – shift the sand – turn over spade or simply swing sideways.
My hill is here,	Swing both hands on one side of the body and bend down deeply at the knees.
Your hill is there,	The same – but now on the other side of the body.
They make a fine pair.	Both arms raised up high.
My hill is high, so very hi-igh.	Stand on tiptoes and stretch your arms high.
Your hill is high, so very hi-igh.	Stretch both arms high and turn them towards another child.
I'm tumbling down, look here,	Lower arms and/or fall down.
Wobble, wobble, wobble...	Digging movements (like a puppy).
Oh dear!	Spread out your arms or think of an alternative.
Here comes a cloud, a big, big clou-oud, Here comes a cloud, a big, big clou-oud.	Stretch your arms out as if you are embracing a big teddy bear.
It's raining on my hill, Tippy, tappy, tat,	Waft hands (slowly at first, then a little faster).
I'm wet.	Shake (water) off hands and buckle knees.

Note: These movements can also be performed sitting on the floor or on a stool.

20

H1

Theme Play

- One or more children are kneeling down on the floor. Their heads are tucked away between their arms. They are sandy hills. We will play Drop the Handkerchief with older pre-school children and infants and when the music has finished there will be a small spade or toy lying behind a child. We can leave out the running away depending on the group.

- The teacher will draw a variety of circles or spots on the floor, or alternatively we can use hoops. Each child sits down in her 'sandy hill' and repeats the actions in the way she chooses.

- The teacher will give a toy or object to one of the children. The child hides it under his clothes. Nobody knows where it is. The actions are carried out freely or as the child perceives them according to the music. During the last notes the child will show his object as a surprise.

- Hiding something can be related to the seasons, for example, in autumn we can hide something under a pile of leaves. Before Christmas we could decorate stockings. We stuff them with other objects and newspaper snippets. The actual present is hidden at the bottom.

- We make a real sand hill in the sand pit outside or in the classroom, and heap more and more sand on it while singing or making noises.

- Finally we sprinkle water over the hill from two wet brushes, imitating rain. If we have hidden an object we can dig for it while singing or saying 'wobble wobble'. Repetition might encourage the children to sing the other words of the song spontaneously.

- We could also make a hill from clay or sweet sticky pudding rice in which we have hidden a couple of raisins. Otherwise we could cover an object in a couple of layers of plaster and when it has hardened we can paint our pieces of art.

The teacher can sing the song with or without the accompaniment of the CD during these actions. It encourages the children to make more movements. It also applies to their expressions on the writing surface. The children could also produce their own sounds during their actions, which personalises their performance. Initially it will not be easy for the teacher to do the actions while singing. That is why we could start by singing 'la-la-la'.

Write Dancing

The children become aware of their sensory and physical means of expression and of contrasts such as up and down, on either side of their bodies, including the contrast between random and focused movements. As soon as these basic movements have become 'second nature' we will consolidate them once again on the writing surface. The actions will remain the same, whether they are performed in their spaces or just above the board as is shown in the Scrimbling suggestions.

H1

Expressions on the Writing Surface

Basic movement: drawing lines from side to side; dots and dashes downwards and upwards

The first song will introduce the children to the coherence between expressions in their spaces and the same expressions on the writing surface. All children can experience it in their own way. The surface area will be a 'land of discovery' where the child is free to explore.

At first we should work with only our fingers on the self-made board (or on a table top). We call it 'finger dancing' which can also be done in shaving foam or in paint. Initially it is best to work on the board with damp sponges, which we squeeze and where we can mess about using our hands, and rub until the surface has dried up again. When the weather is fine we can do this outside which will allow children's little feet to have a go at Write Dance too. As soon as the child begins to feel comfortable with Write Dancing and the music becomes familiar the basic movements will run more smoothly. The process of automatising, which is necessary to be able to write, is set in motion in a playful way. The teacher should not point to 'beautiful' shapes or demonstrate them because the aim is to get children to make coarse motor skill movements and the results are not important. Of course the teacher should join in each time.

Scrimbling: writing movements

On the beach – lots of sa-and,
On the beach – lots of sa-and.

Standing or sitting: waving from side to side with a piece of chalk in both hands.

My hill is here, your hill is there,

1. Draw lines up and down (hill) anywhere on the paper.

2. Draw one, two or more hills.

They make a fine pair.

Pieces of chalk up in the air.

22

2nd verse

My hill is high, so very high,
Your hill is high, so very high.
Tiptoe * and draw lines upwards.

I'm tumbling down, look here,
Back on their feet and lines downwards.

Wobble, wobble, wobble...
1. Drawing circles, drawing lines from side to side.

2. Drawing 'scratchy lines'.

Oh dear!
Arms up.

3rd verse

Here comes a cloud,
A big, big clou-oud.
Drawing circles.

It's raining on my hill,
Dashes and dots everywhere.

Tippy, tappy, tap,
Speckle.

I'm wet.
Powerful rods downwards.

H2

Kringeli-krangeli

Yoyo and Meema have spent the whole day playing on the beach. Now they are on their way home. They shake the sand off their bare bodies and get dressed. They are very tired and their tiny feet find it so difficult walking through the warm sand.

Finally they are on the footpath home. This is much better. Mum, Yoyo and Meema sing the song 'Kringeli-krangeli krongelidong' each time they see a long bend. They walk in a straight line and then from side to side. They like that game and they forget their tiredness after a full day on the beach. Suddenly Meema stops.

'Mum, there is so much sand in my shoe, what shall I do?'

'Shake it,' says Mum, and Meema gives it a good shake. The sand pours out at her toes and her heel.

'It's a good job you are wearing sandals, Meema,' says Yoyo, 'otherwise you would have had to take off your shoes.'

'I can see our house,' says Mum, but they still have quite a way to go. And because the three of them keep on singing it seems to go quicker and suddenly they find they are home again. And who sits down on the pavement?

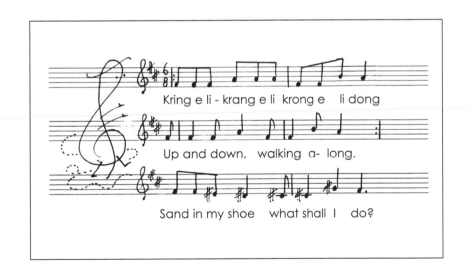

Kringeli-krangeli krongelidong,
Up and down, walking along.
Sand in my shoe what shall I do?
Sand in my shoe what shall I do?
Wobble, wobble, wobble...

Go sand!
Kringeli krangeli krongelidong
Far from home and on we roam
A long long way to go
And then we'll be back home (4x)

H2

Movements

Words	Movements
Kringeli-krangeli krongelidong,	Wriggle your hands and wrists and your whole body.
Up and down,	Hands up in the air, hands straight up or beside your body.
Walking along.	Hands down.
Kringeli-krangeli krongelidong,	Wriggling.
Up and down walking along.	Hands up in the air, hands down.
Sand in my shoe what shall I do?	Put one foot forward. *Sitting down: shake two feet simultaneously.*
Sand in my shoe what shall I do?	Repeat with other foot.
Wobble, wobble, wobble...	Shake one foot or the entire body.
Go sand!	Turn palms up or invent your own variation.
Kringeli-krangeli krongelidong,	Wriggling.
Far from home and on we roam.	Point in the distance with a hand or finger – or repeatedly to the writing surface with a house drawn on it.
Kringeli-krangeli krongelidong,	Wriggling.
Far from home and on we roam.	Pointing.
A long long way to go,	Make long strides down the classroom or in your place. *Sitting down: stamp on the ground.*
And then we'll be back home. (4x)	Jumping or skipping movements or running away and finding a place to sit down.

H2

Theme Play

- Take a piece of chalk and draw a wriggly, bendy 'krongelidong' path across the room or in the playground and let the children follow it.

- Twisting and turning like the krongelidong means twisting and turning in the air or on the ground like a krongelidong animal. A krongelidong animal is an animal we will frequently meet in Write Dance. You can make one out of circular movements and loops: eyes, ears, whiskers and paws, and hey presto! First you twist and turn like the krongelidong with your entire body, lying down or standing up, and then on the writing surface. In the sand you can also twist and turn with your fingers, making tracks and then drawing eyes with your index.

- The teacher will make a fist and press it sideways in the sand. It represents a little child's foot. Next we will press five little toes at the top with our index to complete the little foot. The children copy it. The little feet Write Dance in the sand and the teacher can sing along.

- A child or a cuddly toy lies on a sheet or blanket and other children pull it along twisting and turning in different directions through the hall.

- Try to make a wriggly 'krongelidong' road with a finger puppet on the back of another one.

- We will cut out pictures and stick them onto a big sheet of paper. We will use a writing implement or simply our fingers to wriggle round them to the music along a bendy road. We continue to use different colours over each other. Don't trace but consolidate the shape in your own personal swing and style (see Introduction).

- The children bring their cuddly toys from home. We will spread them around in a large area. Listening to the music we will weave our way round them. When the music stops each child will try and find his own cuddly animal. The children will also wriggle their own animal in the air, far away, close to them, high up in the air or just above the ground.

- As we did in Sandy Hill we can sit down in a hoop, this time with our cuddly animals. It's our little den. When the music begins to play we get up and weave our way around like the krongelidong.

- We fill our shoes with sand in the sandpit and let it all run out again. There is another option, which is to fold a paper cornet, filling it with very fine sand and then cutting off a tiny tip, just like a piping bag. We can use it to make twisty tracks on a tray or on the self-made board. This technique can be applied to all the following themes to make straight lines, waves, circles and semi-circles, arches and boats.

Write Dancing

The swinging movements teach the child to manage changes of direction smoothly. We will do the same with the matching theme My Dinky Car in Funfair. The meandering and round movements contrast with the angular movements which we will practise in The Staircase and The Procession.

Expressions on the Writing Surface

Basic movement: twisting and looped movements across the entire writing surface

'Wriggling', 'twisting' or 'playing krongelidong' are typical Write Dance words. They all mean the same: bending and using the joints in your body. On a writing surface we will do the same with our fingers and hands. We will first allow the children to discover how they can express themselves on a board, paper, in shaving foam or with other materials. One child will do it carefully and another will be wild. Twisting and bending encourages pleasure and flexibility on the writing surface and they all do it in their own way. Most shapes, lines and connections in our handwriting consist of round or rounded writing movements. They encourage speed but often cause most problems in fine motor skills. The more flexible the children manage their bodies, the more natural their basic movements and varieties on the writing surface will be. Once again, it is not the shapes that matter in pre-school Write Dance but the repeated movements.

Tickling and scratching are healthy and make your letters sound and wealthy.

Scrimbling: Writing Movements

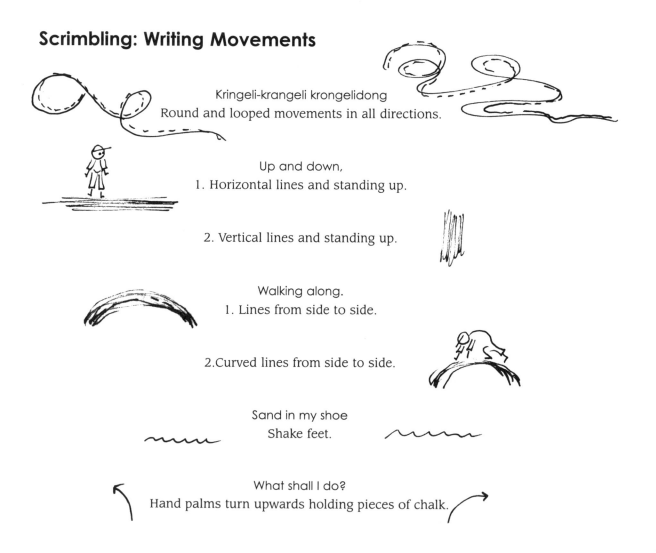

Kringeli-krangeli krongelidong
Round and looped movements in all directions.

Up and down,
1. Horizontal lines and standing up.

2. Vertical lines and standing up.

Walking along.
1. Lines from side to side.

2.Curved lines from side to side.

Sand in my shoe
Shake feet.

What shall I do?
Hand palms turn upwards holding pieces of chalk.

2nd verse

Far from home and on we roam
1. Point a piece of chalk up in the air.

2. Horizontal lines on the writing surface.

(Horizon)

A long long way to go, (2x)
Bent or straight lines (steps).

And then we'll be back home.
Dotting and hopping.

H3

Pat-a-cake

Matching Theme Funfair
Merry-go-round

'Today we will make something easy for lunch,' says Mum, 'how about making a pat-a-cake? Come, let's make the pastry.'

Mum puts butter, flour, eggs and milk in a bowl and Yoyo and Meema take turns stirring with the wooden spoon.

When it is Meema's turn, she sings, 'Stir well, round and round,' but Yoyo won't join in. He tries to get rid of all the lumps by squeezing them with his spoon, but it doesn't always work.

Mum gives him the mixer. 'Tap-tap-tap-tap,' says the mixer hitting the bowl. And the pastry is ready. Now they've got to grease the baking tin. Yoyo's butter slips on the floor. Meema is more careful and finishes the job. She has done it very nicely, without making a mess. Clever Meema.

Yoyo is very hungry and can't wait, so he takes a big spoonful out of the tin. Mum is very cross. Meema and Yoyo go to play while the cake is in the oven. After an hour they come back to taste the cake.

Meema gives a piece of cake to her two favourite dolls, she pretends they are siblings.

'I have eaten a third piece,' says Yoyo, but Meema has left hers, because she is no longer hungry and prefers to play.

'And now off to bed,' says Mum. But Yoyo and Meema don't feel tired. Dad plays a game with them on the stairs: one-and-two-and-three…!

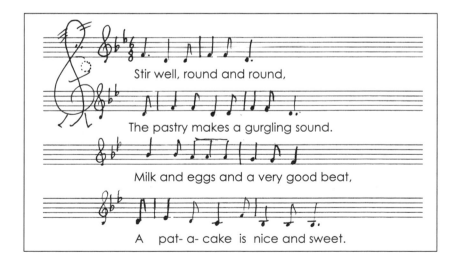

Stir well, round and round,
The pastry makes a gurgling sound.
Milk and eggs and a very good beat,
A pat-a-cake is nice and sweet.

Stir well, round and round,
One for my mum and one for my gran.
Yum yum yum and tum tum tum,
My pat-a-cake is down in my tum.

H3

Movements

Words	Movements
Stir well round and round,	Stirring movements with your hands and whole body.
The pastry makes a gurgling sound.	Repeat.
Milk and eggs and a very good beat,	Make a big circle with both arms, or neck or nose. *Sitting down: with your feet.*
A pat-a-cake is nice and sweet.	Put in mouth.
Stir well, round and round,	Stretch out one hand or point at a boy.*
One for my mum * (you)	Stretch out other hand or point at a girl.*
And one for my gran.* (me)	Pretend to eat the cake.
Yum yum yum and tum tum tum My pat-a-cake is down in my tum.	Finally turn the hand palms up.

H3

Theme Play

- The children stir within a hoop, and then lie down in or on the hoop and turn round and round as if they were a cake in a tin.

- We will spray enough shaving cream on a big piece of plastic to enable us to make a cake with round movements. The children are given a wet cloth and grease the tin by swirling the cloth to the left and to the right.

- Make circular or rounded movements with different parts of the body; hands, arms, legs, head, stomach... while sitting or lying down. In winter we could imagine making snowballs. We pretend to be snowballs by rolling about in the classroom or making the snowballs out of little balls of paper.

- Draw a circle on the floor with a piece of chalk and walk on the line with the children following you. Ask the children to erase the line with a brush or another cleaning instrument.

- Walking, twisting or dancing in the classroom: when the music is set to 'pause' all the children stand in the circle; when the music plays, they disperse.

- Making pastry for a pie: the children stir in turns while singing the song. Baking cakes could be another activity.

Write Dancing

We experience round movements and shapes contrary to the angular movements and shapes in The Staircase and The Procession. The gentle waltz theme evokes calm and safe feelings. Going round in circles is a continuous movement that can be repeated infinitely, in any direction, first with both hands, then alternating hands.

33

H3

Expressions on the Writing Surface

Basic movement: rotating or circular movements

Some children like scribbling and 'scrimbling' with complete abandon in all directions of the writing surface. Others prefer straighter lines, although we may also see spontaneous circling developing on the writing surface. When a child is a little older we will see a tendency to draw shapes, whereas moving freely on the writing surface remains an essential prerequisite. The teacher should continue to encourage this rounded 'scrimbling'. Drawing circles or 'swimming' with both hands on the writing surface is important because it encourages smooth and fluent movements. Letters consist of round and straight movements and shapes. Straight lines usually don't cause any difficulties in the field of fine motor skills. Round lines, rounded lines or bent changes of direction are a different matter. These bends often become forced, due to inadequate motor skills or compensation, and are written with too much force. The joined up letters show irregular angles and unintentional strokes. Recurrent repetition of rounded basic movements and circles relaxes children. Natural relaxation is stored in the brain and eases the handwriting. 'Scrimbling in circles' is very important.

Scrimbling: Writing Movements

Stir well, round and round,
The pastry makes a gurgling sound.
1. Draw one or two circles with both hands in the same direction

2. In the opposite direction.

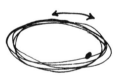

Milk and eggs and a very good beat,

1. Random dots.

2. Drawing four dots to the rhythm.

A pat-a-cake is nice and sweet.
More scrimbling in circles.

2nd verse

Stir well, round and round,
Scrimbling in circles.

One for my mum (you) and one for my gran (me).
Using different colours in the existing circles.

Yum yum yum and tum tum tum,
My pat-a-cake is down in my tum.

Draw dots to the rhythm or freely.

H4

The Staircase

'Come on Yoyo and Meema, don't dally, off to bed,' says Dad. 'Do you know what we will do, we will count the steps. How many steps are there Meema?' Meema doesn't know.

Dad shows her what to do. He sets one foot on the first step and counts out loud. Yoyo and Meema follow him.

'One,' says Dad.

'Two,' says Yoyo.

'Three,' says Meema.

'Four,' says Mum, standing at the bottom of the stairs. And suddenly Pippa the cat runs upstairs taking big leaps.

'She has forgotten to count,' exclaims Dad. But cats can't count anyway, or do you think they can?

'I don't want to go to bed yet,' says Meema and she quickly runs down all the steps. Yoyo copies her.

'Alright, just a short play, is that okay Mum?' Dad asks. That's fine and they have a really fun time. Meema takes a big leap when she reaches the bottom step.

'I can take two in one go,' says Meema and she shows them.

'And I can take three,' says Dad and the three of them get very excited.

'Now you should really go to bed,' Mum shouts from the kitchen, and they count the remaining steps.

Seven, eight and nine and ten, one final jump and Yoyo is back up again.

'Did you see that jump, Dad?'

'Yes and it was a clever one,' says Dad, and now off to bed and then we will sing the song once more.

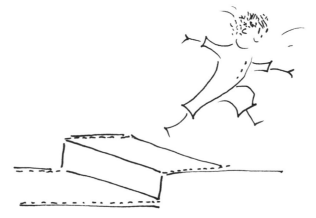

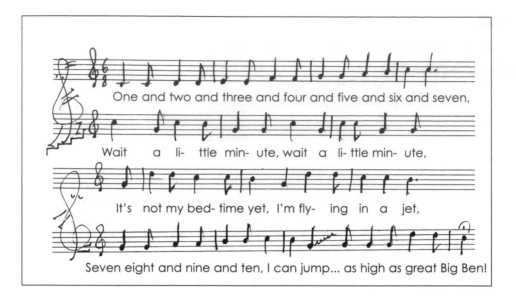

One and two and three and four and five and six and seven,
Wait a little minute,
Wait a little minute,
I haven't moved an inch,
A teeny weenie pinch,
Seven eight and nine and ten,
I can jump...
As high as great Big Ben! (4x)

H4

Movements

Words	Movements
One and two and three and four and five and six and seven,	Pretend climbing stairs to the rhythm.
Wait a little minute, Wait a little minute,	Stand still.
It's not my bedtime yet, I'm flying in a jet,	Slowly shake your head.
Seven eight and nine and ten	Walk up the stairs.
I can jump...	A big jump forward. *Sitting down: 'jump' with your feet.*
As high as great Big Ben! (4x)	Alternate turning hand palms upwards and downwards.
One and two and three and four and five and six and seven,	Walk up the stairs.
Wait a little minute, Wait a little minute,	Stand still.
I haven't moved an inch,	Stand still holding arms down alongside body.
A teeny weenie pinch,	Stand still as stiff as a board.
Seven eight and nine and ten,	Walk up the stairs.
I can jump...	Big jump forward. *Sitting down: 'jump' with your feet.*
As high as great Big Ben! (4x)	Turn hand palms upwards and downwards.

H4

Theme Play

- The teacher beats the drum slowly and the children take big slow steps. We can imagine ourselves going upstairs. Can we count slowly while we are doing it? Next we take a big jump or a very small one: variation creates suppleness in body, mind and on the writing surface.

- A fast beat on the drum: The children walk quickly (running up and down the stairs).

- The drum stops: The children stop dead (stopping halfway up the stairs). Alternate a couple of times. We could also attach bells to their feet to reinforce the movements.

- Draw big and small lines, we take a big stride when we see a big line and a small step when we come to a small line.

    * Can we walk step by step, inch by inch?

    * Big jumps and little jumps.

- A staircase is angular; we look for angular objects or name them. Make a game with sharp and round objects. The children sit down in a circle with a round sheet over their laps. Unfamiliar round objects are passed round and named. We will do the same with a sheet held tight and angular objects.

Write Dancing

The rhythm of the march will give children a sense of time and beat. This is how set or taut movements and feelings will be felt and confirmed. The regular or 'set' rhythm helps us emphasise the control of physical co-ordination. Contrary to swinging and round movements these movements are interrupted intentionally and succeeded by another movement.

H4

Expressions on the Writing Surface

Basic movement: straight and angular movements and lines

It is easier for a child to make angular movements than round ones because the simplest link between two dots is a straight line. Very often they use too much force, particularly when it only concerns one line. Moving from side to side 'makes the brain accustomed' to these movements and eventually they will not need to be done by will power. They will have been stored in the 'hardware' and can emerge naturally, provided they have been practised or consolidated sufficiently. Using strength or force requires a lot of energy and a child will tire quickly or lose interest in colouring or writing. Drawing lines from side to side is a rudimentary movement. They may show a slight curve. Sucking and kicking, and the first reflexive movements sideways are survival motions. Impulsive strokes upward or downward, which we might see in the signatures of young children, might point to 'remnants' of these rudimentary reflexes and can be overcome with motor skill training by renewing movements sideways. Upright or vertical lines either go towards or from the body. They are a little more unnatural to the child than horizontal lines and therefore need to be learnt and programmed into the brain. The ability to switch spontaneously from angles to rounded lines promotes spring and elasticity in their handwriting. Letters actually consist of round and straight shapes only. In Write Dance experiencing and trying basic movements and combinations that lie hidden in shapes always precedes writing. Teacher and children can first try the actions to sounds and noises or by counting, and finally to music.

Scrimbling: Writing Movements

One and two and three and four and five and six and seven,
1. Lines from side to side.

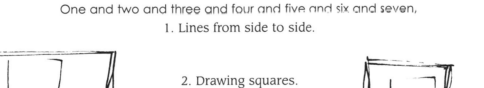

2. Drawing squares.

3. Angular movements to draw the squares.

Wait a little minute, (2x)
Hold pieces of chalk up high.

It's not my bedtime yet,
I'm flying in a jet,
Draw lines from side to side and simultaneously shake your head.

Seven eight and nine and ten,
Drawing dots and lines.

I can jump...
As high as great Big Ben!
Make a big arched jump like a flea.

2nd verse

I haven't moved an inch,
A teeny weeny pinch,
Straighten your back and hold pieces of chalk still.

H5

The Toy Train

Matching Theme Funfair:

Air Train

It is Yoyo's birthday and he has been given a wooden train. It is a beautiful train, the carriages are red and the engine has yellow lines along the side.

'This train has travelled all the way from toy land,' Grandpa said, when Yoyo unpacked the present.

Meema and Yoyo play with the train and its five carriages. The doors can open and close. It isn't difficult to assemble the tracks. Yoyo and Meema have laid them in a nice circle. It means the train can continue to run round and round. It runs smoothly over the track. Meema likes the gentle sound when Yoyo pushes it along carefully.

'I wouldn't mind being that train myself,' says Meema. 'I would carry everybody wherever they want to go across the world.'

Yoyo stops and suddenly shouts, 'Now we are at a station, please descend.'

'What's the name of the station?' asks Meema, but Yoyo doesn't know, he is too busy opening and closing the doors. Meema thinks of a cute name, can you imagine which one?

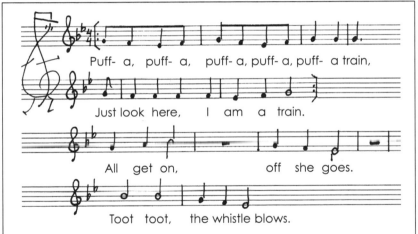

Puffa, puffa, puffa, puffa, puffa train,
Just look here, I am a train.
Puffa, puffa, puffa, puffa, puffa train,
Here we're going through the rain.
Just a mo,
Rightee-ho!
We are ready, off we go.

H5

Movements

Words	Movements
Puffa, puffa, puffa, puffa, puffa train,	Turn round arms parallel to the body like an old-fashioned train and follow each other in a line.
Just look here, I am a train.	Stop dead and continue turning arms.
Puffa, puffa, puffa, puffa, puffa train,	Train movements (walking).
Here we're going through the rain.	Train movements (stationary).
All get on,	One step forward.*
Off she goes.	One step back or turn round and take a step *.
Toot toot, the whistle blows.	Pull an imaginary whistle with one hand.
Puffa, puffa, puffa, puffa, puffa train,	Train movements (walking).
Just look here, I am a train.	Train movements (stationary).
Puffa, puffa, puffa, puffa, puffa train,	Train movements (walking).
Here we're going through the rain.	Train movements (stationary).
Just a mo,	Remain stationary. The arms are motionless too.
Rightee-ho!	The arms remain motionless.
We are ready, off we go.	Walk among the crowd and wave.

H5

Theme Play

- Follow each other through the classroom like a train, swinging the arms forward in line with each other and backward in a similar fashion. It is also possible to take a piece of chalk and draw a train track on the floor. We can make some marks with confetti, snippets of paper or by spreading sand. We travel through the field of marks in our train. It is also possible to express this on a writing surface. If something is knocked over by accident and makes a mark, we could in future pass by in the 'cloth or mark train' to tidy up the 'marked area', if you like while singing the song.

- Sitting down on the floor or on a long bench continue to swing the arms round in line with each other or casually above your head. Set the music to pause. The arms have stopped moving, the music continues and the arms turn backward. We can also do this while walking.

- Pretend to be a train by lining up chairs behind each other.

- Move arms horizontally away from each other and towards each other, like smoke or making the movement of turning wheels. Both hands and wrists make looped movements. We reinforce the actions with ribbons, scarves or strips of crepe paper.

- We sit down on the floor with our legs stretched forward.

Puffa puffa	The arms turn
All get on	Open legs
Off she goes	Close legs
Toot toot, the whistle blows	Draw knees up to stomach

- Place small items in a line on the floor, first walk round them in loops and then allow them to draw on floor with chalk.

  Upward (garlands)  or downward (arches).

- The song is sung by the teacher and the children with or without the CD; alternatively we first make some noises to get the feel of the movements and to alternate them.

Write Dancing

Arms turning in circles give a sense of continuity. Speed, fun and a feeling for opposites are developed by first pronouncing 'puffa puffa' slowly and then more quickly. The train can move forwards or backwards. We may also repeat moving and stopping with other sounds. We could also imagine other vehicles that could carry us.

H5

Expressions on the Writing Surface

Basic movement: round movements pushing themselves along and becoming loops

The round arm movements belonging to this song are expressed on the writing surface in loops, upwards or downwards. We need these basic looped join ups in cursive writing. They are made by joining up semi-circles in loops. The contrasts of arched loops downwards 〰️ and garland loops 𝓮𝓮𝓮 upwards stimulate the brain signals and they are a prerequisite for flowing and easy handwriting. The alternation of loops at the top and at the bottom in handwriting, as well as the alternation of m-shaped and u-shaped join ups, can be difficult for the young learner. Drawing loops along an imaginary line is a necessary and healthy exercise to help a smooth learning process of handwriting and it is one we can perform in any direction. Random 'scribbling' is innate to all small children and giving them a line to follow in a playful way is a push in the right writing direction, but it also depends on the child's interest. First we will accompany this 'train scrimbling' with sounds and noises and then it will be repeated with music.

Scrimbling: Writing Movements

 Puffa, puffa, puffa, puffa, puffa train,
Just look here, I am a train (2x)
1. Draw loops in all directions

2. Circling round

 All get on,
1. Draw dots or circle around on the same spot.

2. Place dots inside the circle.

Off she goes.
1. Place dots in a line.
2. Draw lines outward.

(Or from side to side which initially tends to be easier.)

Toot toot, the whistle blows.
Draw lines downward.

2nd verse

Just a mo,
Rightee-ho!
Circling around or lift chalk off the paper.

We are ready, off we go.
Draw dots, dashes or 'little people'.

Tickle Tree

Autumn has arrived in Yoyo's and Meema's garden. Dad has swept up a whole pile of leaves. There are acorns all over the ground and Meema fetches a bucket for them. Yoyo gets his little rake and rakes more leaves towards the big pile. The leaves fly in all directions and Yoyo throws himself onto the big heap. He takes off his coat and the leaves tickle him everywhere in his neck, in his hair, between his fingers, on his legs, everywhere. He really enjoys rolling around and he has almost flattened the pile of leaves. Meema's bucket is nearly full. She only picks up acorns with little caps and leaves the others. Then she begins to roll in the leaves, but keeps on her jacket so that the leaves can't tickle her.

Yoyo invents a funny little game.

'You know what, Meema, I will throw up the leaves and you've got to catch them, okay?'

He takes a big lump of leaves in both hands. Meema grabs in all directions. It isn't easy at all. Her hands try to catch.

'I've got a chestnut,' she cries out with delight. It is a beauty and so shiny. She puts it in her pocket. The rain begins to fall gently, so they go indoors. What will they be playing?

Leaves and leaves they tickle,

Hands and fin- gers pri- ckle,

Snatch it, look here, snatch,

Watch it, try and catch.

Watch the acorns tumble,
Acorns they roll and rumble,
Snatch it, look here, snatch,
Watch it, try and catch.

H6

Movements

Leaves and leaves they tickle, Hands and fingers prickle,	Shake entire body and wriggle hands and fingers.
Snatch it, look here, snatch,	Stretch out both arms in turn.
Watch it try and catch.	Continue to stretch out arms and make snatch and catch movements
Watch the acorns tumble,	Arms stretched forward and then allowed to drop.
Acorns they roll and rumble,	Allowing arms to drop further and bend knees deeply. Sitting down: drop arms and let head rest in lap.
Snatch it, look here, snatch, Watch it, try and catch.	Stretch out arms, make snatch and catch movements.

H6

Theme Play

- Tickle your own body or somebody else's, with fingers, finger puppets, combs or anything you can think of. Alternate between rubbing face, arms and feet with cotton wool to sense the soft feeling in contrast, or… go and tickle the teacher, all of you.

- Make a pile of leaves in autumn to play in. We could also put some crisps or soft biscuits in a plastic bag and crumble them entirely. Spread the crumbs out on a big cloth, take a straw and blow them together in a big heap.

- Move hands and fingers in shaving foam and scrimble. Use a pipette to add coloured drops. They could represent acorns in need of a wash.

- Make snatching movements while blindfolded or under a sheet to encourage the feeling sensation: pick chestnuts, acorns, branches and strong leaves out of a basket, name them and put them on the table.

- The teacher and the children discuss trees and woods. How do trees stand, straight or perpendicular, close or far apart, against a wall or in a big field? Children think of varieties and depict them. In this way we experience big and small, low and high, thick and thin, earth and sky. What do trees need in order to grow, what do trees look like in winter and in summer? Roll chestnuts and other autumn products on a sheet or cloth and 'play' with them by moving the cloth up and down. Stop the chestnuts and let them rest, they are tired of playing.

Write Dancing

Alternating focused and random movements, lines and dots. It is about the pleasure the child derives from Write Dancing. Some children scrimble their names in their own way which reinforces their self-confidence. After all it is not about results.

Expressions on the Writing Surface

Basic movement: lines, dots and free movements

In this song we first make tickle and shake movements and then we do the snatch actions. The music clearly indicates what we need to do, but to many children the music is no more than a noise in the background and it will take some time before eye-hand-ear co-ordination takes off. Don't forget the sounds and noises. Everything is derived from movement, as in nature itself, so real life drawings of trees are not appropriate during the scrimbling phase. The teacher might like to illustrate something while 'scrimbling'. Making dots causes a lot of noise and is a fun activity. We could consciously interrupt this noise for a welcome change by ringing a little bell and then continue, which will turn it into a focused listening exercise.

Scrimbling: Writing Movements

Leaves and leaves they tickle,
1. Shake whole body.

2. Let the crayons shake on the writing surface.

Hands and fingers prickle,
Possibly hold fingers and crayons above the writing surface and continue to wobble

Snatch it, look here, snatch,
Watch it, try and catch.
1. Draw dots and dashes.

2. Draw circles.

2nd verse

Watch the acorns tumble,
Acorns they roll and rumble,
Draw dots or circles over each other or draw hasty small circles.

Snatch it, look here, snatch,
Watch it, try and catch.
Big dots.

H7

Little Water Shute

Matching Theme Funfair:
Big Water Shute

Yoyo and Meema assemble their plastic slide in the bathroom. There are very many big and small pieces to make the slide into a real rolling shute. It is not an easy job but Yoyo knows exactly what to do and has a serious look on his face. The water shute is ready.

'Is it in the right position Meema?' he asks, and moves it a little more towards the centre of the table. The bottom part of the shute is now hanging over the edge of the bath. Meema has filled the bath with a bit of water and picks up her bucket full of acorns. She draws faces on them.

'The little acorn men can really swim,' she says. In a blue bucket she pours lots of water over the slide and she lets the acorn men tumble down one after the other. When they fall on the floor off the slide it makes them laugh. There are also acorns that do land in the bath and Meema makes high waves with her hands. They all continue to float but they lose their faces. Mum comes upstairs and sees the bathroom.

'It looks like a real swimming pool,' she says. The whole floor is wet. They dry everything up with towels and the slide can stay up till the following day.

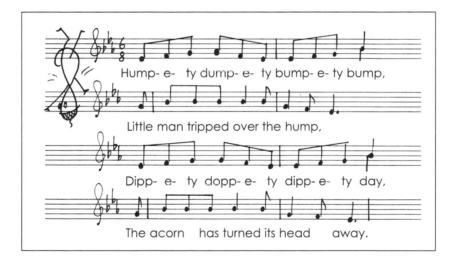

Hump- e- ty dump- e- ty bump- e- ty bump,

Little man tripped over the hump,

Dipp- e- ty dopp- e- ty dipp- e- ty day,

The acorn   has turned its head   away.

Tickety tackety tickety tack,
The little man's lying on his back,
Bippety boppety bippety ben,
The acorn has turned round again.

H7

Movements

Words	Movements
Humpety dumpety bumpety bump,	Make wavy movements with your arms up in the air and sway from side to side sitting or standing.
Little man tripped over the hump,	Bend head down and rub it with round movements.
Dippety doppety dippety day,	Make wavy movements with your arms and sway, turn wrists upwards on 'day'.
The acorn has turned its head away.	Tap palm of one hand with fingers of the other hand, possibly with an acorn.
Tickety tackety tickety tack,	Wave arms and/or sway entire body. On 'tack' sit down on floor and fall gently on your back.
The little man's lying on his back,	Remain on back or roll from side to side.
Bippety boppety bippety ben,	Rise up slowly, spread arms up in the air or simply turn wrists upward.
The acorn has turned round again.	Once again tap palm with fingers or an acorn.

54

H7

Theme Play

- Place building bricks or boxes behind each other with approximately one metre between them. Hold a hose or a rope together with the children and weave in and out between the objects. Next all the children weave through in turn or in pairs. The end of the rope may drag over the ground so that the other children can see how to create a wavy movement.

- While walking along we spread our arms out like wings and occasionally bend our knees to fly 'high' and 'low'. We can imagine ourselves to be flying birds, snakes, dragons or horses. The more imagination, the better.

- Just relax lying on the floor listening to the sounds or move along crawling like waves.

- A couple of children hold a plastic tablecloth by the edges. The teacher puts a little water on it and a piece of crepe paper. We can rock the cloth gently to the music and the crepe paper will colour the water.

- A couple of children will hold onto an old sheet. A couple of objects are laid on the sheet and it is moved slightly. A child will creep under the sheet and enjoy the 'shadow play'.

- Ask the children to cut coloured paper circles (buy stickers or make them yourself) in halves. They should stick them side by side; a round side up and a round side down, and then use a writing implement to draw the wavy movements along them. 'Humpety dumpety bumpety bump' is sung or recited in a variety of sounds and then played with the music. Alternatively all kinds of cuddly toys can be cut out of magazines, stuck on paper with krongelidong and train loops or wavy humpety dumpety movements drawn round them. Don't forget the sounds or switch on the music.

Write Dancing

Once again these movements help children to experience smooth transitions. The music of The Staircase or The Procession helps to clarify the different feelings belonging to angles, and the movements can be performed in their space or on a writing surface. The teacher and the children discuss water, wet and dry, ships and boats and we could pretend to swim on the floor or roll about in the imaginary waves. We talk about high and low waves and blow the way the wind goes, from very gentle to very forceful, for example, against a candle flame or a feather.

H7

Expressions on the Writing Surface

Basic movement: wavy movements in all directions from side to side

Rolling movements and lines can be achieved by moving two semi-circles along a line. A circle is given a 'top' and a 'bottom'. Top and bottom and left and right are concepts that a pre-school child cannot yet distinguish. We could regard their tops as arches (closed) and their bottoms as garlands or boats (open). The 'arch' concept is still a difficult one for very young children. Show a variety of pictures which enables them to imagine and combine, if possible using The Gateway from Funfair. Like we did when we were making 'train loops' we are learning how to make contrasts change into flowing lines. The brain is automatised, or in other words 'it just gets used to it' which will encourage fantasy and the ability to be expressed.

There aren't any hidden letters, except when you draw waves in a standing or vertical position. It makes a good 'start' for letter 's'. Waves symbolically match emotions, feelings and spheres. The more variety in wavy movements, the more liveliness and expression of emotions you will see in a child. The brain sometimes finds straight lines 'boring'; a bit of 'swell' is welcome.

Scrimbling: Writing Movements

Humpety dumpety bumpety bump,
Waves from side to side.

Little man tripped over the hump,
1. Waves from side to side.

2. Draw circles.

3. Draw dots.

Dippety doppety dippety day,
The acorn has turned its head away.
Waves and dots.

2nd verse

Tickety tackety tickety tack,
The little man's lying on his back
Swaying or making 'boat' movements.

Bippety boppety bippety ben,
The acorn has turned round again.
Waves and possibly circling round.

Turn the music up and down and try to make the movements bigger and smaller in accordance.

H8

The Rainbow

Yoyo and Meema are playing in the garden; they are playing cat and mouse. Yoyo is the cat and Meema is the mouse. Meema can run very fast and keeps hiding behind the bushes. Yoyo doesn't like it, he can't find her anywhere.

'I won't play anymore,' he shouts at the top of his voice until Meema finally reappears.

'Okay, shall we play another game?' asks Meema. Yoyo wants to be the lion and creeps through the bushes. Pippa, the cat, thinks it is fun and keeps up with him.

'You must roar, don't forget,' says Meema, 'because I am a little lion cub and otherwise I will lose you.' Yoyo is very good at roaring and the lady next door peeps over the hedge to see what is going on. She has two ice creams in paper cups with umbrellas on top. What a nice surprise!

'Here you are, little roaring lions,' she says, 'here are two ice creams for you, they were left over.'

'Thank you very much,' they both say and sit down in the grass with their ice creams.

'Look this is a parasol,' says Meema. In hot countries they use parasols because the sun burns. This is what she has learnt at school. She points her parasol upwards.

'No, you're wrong, it's raining Meema, the grass is getting wet,' says Yoyo. How is that possible? Where has the rain suddenly come from?

'Look up quickly,' says the neighbour, 'there's a rainbow.' What beautiful bright colours!

But it is beginning to pour and Yoyo and Meema run inside. They look for shawls in the dressing-up box, because now they want to play rainbows. Can you imagine how they will play rainbows?

Red and blue
And green and violet,
Now look here, my jacket is wet
Many colours, long and wide,
I am swaying left and right.
Look at the rainbow up in the sky, so high, let's fly,
Away up in the sky. (4x)

H8

Movements

Words	Movements
Red and yellow Blue and indigo,	Hands/wrists make arched movements.
Here comes the rain and there goes the sun.	Turn wrists, palms upwards.
Many colours, long and wide, I am swaying left and right.	Arched movements with arms and entire body.
Look at the rainbow up in the sky, so high, let's fly,	Standing on their toes * and stretching their arms up high.
Away up in the sky.(4x)	Looking up and jumping around. Sitting down: make heel to toe movements with feet.
Red and blue and green and violet,	Now look here, my jacket is wet.
Many colours, long and wide, I am swaying left and right.	Pull one or two scarves tightly between both arms and make arches.
Look at the rainbow up in the sky, so high, let's fly,	On their toes, arms up.
Away up in the sky. (4x)	Look up and wave their scarves.

H8

Theme Play

- We walk up and down the hall or stamp our feet while sitting down; when the teacher rings a bell, the children wave their arms high up in the air. We could also first rock our heads from side to side, followed by our hands and next with our entire body. We can do this either standing, sitting or lying down.

- Two children form an arch holding their hands against each other. We play games by walking or crawling under the arches.

- One child represents the rainbow by making an arch with her body down to the ground. The other children place the scarves on top of her one by one.

- The teacher draws a big arch on the self-made boards and the children wipe out their arches with movements from side to side, wet or dry.

- Draw little umbrellas, cut them out and stick them onto a stick.

- You might be able to buy some mesh 'food umbrellas', which protect food from flies. Cover them with a scarf and hide objects under them (arch = closed, hidden). Turn over the umbrella and put light objects in it, and if you like allow it to float in an inflatable swimming pool (boat = openness, free to pick up again). We can also hang an umbrella from a pulley from the ceiling to lay objects in it and thus hide them. We will take them out when we lower the umbrella. You could also invent guessing games.

- Play outside with garden hose and umbrella.

Write Dancing

This theme helps emphasise arched movements, contrary to Watermill in Funfair where we emphasise the rocking or swaying boat movements. We will use many colours, both in our space and on a writing surface. Which sounds can we make to accompany the 'arched' movements to bring out the effects strongly? And which ones go with the 'boat' movements? Of course we will also discuss the weather and our clothes, and wet and dry materials. When do we see the rainbow in the sky?

H8

Expressions on the Writing Surface

Basic movement: arches from side to side

We can create arched movements by placing semi-circles in a row on a line with their round sides up.

'Arches' are 'closed' movements or shapes.

An arch contains a natural degree of tension and has a supporting, yet also a protective feel. When it rains you protect yourself with an umbrella, when the sun is bright you put up a parasol. However, the 'garland' and the 'boat' have an open feel.

Contrary to the arch the garland hangs loosely, and you can sit in a boat and allow yourself to sway from side to side. You can drink from a bowl or a cup and mouths open and tongues relax.

We write from left to right. If a child has not experienced the essential swaying movements well enough, writing in the required direction might cause problems. We can see it happen in the reversal of letters, distortions, shaky letters, strokes upwards or downwards and unnecessary compensations.

In Write Dance we first make semi-arches while working on the corresponding theme 'Cats', followed by some arches which can be developed into ocean waves or beach waves.

Scrimbling: Writing Movements

Red and yellow
Blue and indigo,

1. Arches from side to side on the same spot.

2. Moving in your space.

The arches (pieces of chalk) can touch each other in opposite directions.

Here comes the rain and there goes the sun.

1. Spots of rain over the arch.

2. Sunray dashes towards the arch.

Look at the rainbow up in the sky, so high, let's fly,

1. Holding the pieces of chalk in their hands they make big arches
with their arms up in the air.

2. Draw bigger arches on the writing surface.

Away up in the sky. (4x)
Draw little lines upwards and look up.

2nd verse

Red and blue
And green and violet,
Only use these colours.

H9

Little Sun

Dear Sun, Dear Moon

It has stopped raining and Yoyo and Meema want to go out into the garden to play.

'Just look at that enormous puddle,' says Yoyo and he begins to stamp in it with his bare feet.

'Splash, splash!' says Yoyo and at first Meema jumps away, but then she joins in. What a lot of fun they are having and it makes them feel quite hot. The sun is coming out again and the sunrays tickle their faces. Now they are splashing about with their hands in the water and the water feels nice and warm too.

'Thank you dear sun,' says Meema, 'for warming up the water. Keep on shining because maybe we will be able to go to the beach tomorrow.' It has rained heavily.

They take a stick and stir in the puddle and make all kinds of wriggly tracks in the wet soil. Yoyo also draws some straight lines and turns the puddle into a little sun. Meema is feeling too hot and finds a new puddle in the shade of the trees.

'Look Yoyo, a little worm,' she calls out. A tiny worm is wriggling in the water and it climbs up Meema's stick. Pippa, the cat, has also seen it. She is playing in the water with her paw but she can't get hold of the worm.

'Come here, put on these hats,' says Mum, and she brings out a red and a blue hat. The sun feels quite hot.

'I am going to fold a hat out of paper,' says Yoyo. Yesterday he learnt how to make one at school. Meema puts a plastic bowl on her head because she likes it more than her hat.

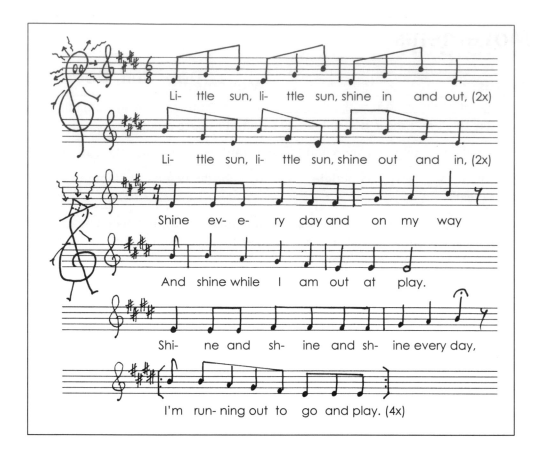

H9

Movements

Words	Movements
Little sun, little sun, shine in and out, Little sun, little sun, shine in and out,	We move our arms away from our body, into the space around us.
Little sun, little sun, shine out and in, Little sun, little sun, shine out and in,	We then 'draw the sunrays towards us' in the opposite direction.
Shine every day and on my way, And shine while I am out at play.	Stretch your arms above your head and bend them. Let your hands gently come down on your head.
Shine and shine and shine every day,	Rub your head.
I'm running out to go and play. (4x)	Everybody runs off and the teacher tries to catch the children. *Sitting down: stamp feet remaining stationary.*

H9

Theme Play

- Represent sunrays beaming out and in while standing, lying down or sitting. We can also try to breathe in and out as long as possible.

- Draw a circle on the floor and when the music is set to 'pause' we walk into the circle.

- Place a tea light in the centre of the circle or on a table. We will discover the distance to the source of heat.

- Try and invent all kinds of games with a child standing in the centre. If you have a Write Dance table (see Introduction) then this should be an appropriate theme for using it.

- Make sunrays inward and outward with paint, shaving foam, bath foam and so on.

- Make a variety of headgear out of newspapers, plastic, cardboard or material and try and express it in the song.

Write Dancing

The alternating movements outward and inward help us experience self-centred feelings towards other people and towards ourselves or giving attention and receiving it. Sucking and blowing prepare you for good inhalation and exhalation.

H9

Expressions on the Writing Surface

Basic movement: moving outward and inward from a central point or a circle

We could also call this theme 'circle of rays' or 'little star'. The alternation between straight and round is something we will also experience in the following theme. It is easy to combine these two themes. Making spirals or simply circling around is something we can do centre inward as well as centre outward. Straight lines from a central point become longer or shorter. In this theme we also experiment with distances and spatial experiences.

Do watch that the children are not too busy drawing simple lines or shapes, but also continue to scrimble. Consolidating using colours, i.e. drawing lines over each other in different colours, giving them your own swing, can continue to stimulate the teacher.

Scrimbling: Writing Movements

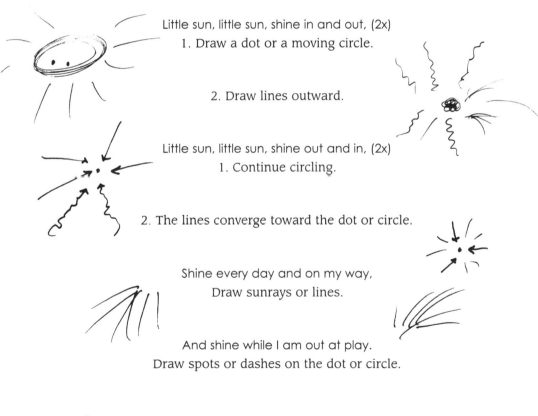

Little sun, little sun, shine in and out, (2x)
1. Draw a dot or a moving circle.

2. Draw lines outward.

Little sun, little sun, shine out and in, (2x)
1. Continue circling.

2. The lines converge toward the dot or circle.

Shine every day and on my way,
Draw sunrays or lines.

And shine while I am out at play.
Draw spots or dashes on the dot or circle.

Shine and shine and shine every day,
Spots and dashes on the point or circle.

I'm running out to go and play. (4x)
Draw spots and dashes everywhere

H10

Straight, Bent, Cross, Happy

Yoyo and Meema are playing on their grandma's and grandpa's big terrace. Yoyo has found a branch of willow. He is the leader of the brass band. His strides are stiff and he waves his branch from side to side.

'Tootah toot toot,' shouts Meema with her hands to her mouth. The branch becomes weak and gives with all the waving about.

'I don't like this game anymore,' says Yoyo.

'Yes Yoyo, look, you can turn it into a complete circle; now it is a hoop.' Meema holds both ends close together and shows him.

'Shall we play circus? You are a puppy, just jump through.' Yoyo jumps and falls flat on his face. He cries and is very cross with Meema.

'Now my branch has snapped completely,' he says angrily and he runs away quickly and stamps his feet.

But a minute later he is back again and says, 'I want to be a brass band leader.' He puts on Grandpa's cap which is lying on a chair. Meema gathers small branches with leaves and quickly picks some daisies on the lawn.

'And look I am one of those girls with a short skirt, waving lots of feathers around.' She cheerfully hops and skips around the garden, but Yoyo continues to step sedately, keeping his back and arms very stiff and meanwhile looking for a new branch.

My back is very straight,

My back is very straight,

My back is very straight,

My back is straight, straight, straight.

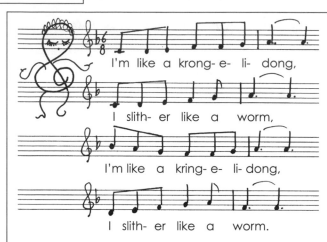

I'm like a krong- e- li- dong,

I slith- er like a worm,

I'm like a kring- e- li- dong,

I slith- er like a worm.

I am so cross, so ve- ry cross,

I am so cross, so ve- ry cross,

I am so cross, so very cross,

I am so cross, cross, cross, cross.

I am so ve- ry ha- ppy, as ha- ppy as can be.

Catch me, catch me, if you can, dance a dance, a dance with me.

I am so ve- ry ha- ppy, as ha- ppy as can be.

Catch me, catch me, if you can, dance along with me.

H10

Movements

Words	Movements
My back is very straight, My back is very straight, My back is very straight, My back is straight, straight, straight.	We are walking with straight backs, hands held tightly against our body or straight up in the air. **no.19 instr.20**
I'm like a krongelidong, I slither like a worm, I'm like a kringelidong, I slither like a worm.	The teacher first shows what 'krongelidong' means: anything that can bend - arms, wrists, ankles, knees, neck, back, if possible everything at the same time. The children copy. **no.21 instr.22**
I am so cross, so very cross, I am so cross, so very cross, I am so cross, so very cross, I am so cross, cross, cross, cross.	We pull angry faces, clench angry fists and stamp down the hall, or stamp while sitting down, to the rhythm of the music. **no.23 instr.24**
I'm so very happy, As happy as can be. Catch me, catch me, if you can, Dance a dance a dance with me. I'm so very happy, As happy as can be. Catch me, catch me, if you can, Dance along with me.	We hop and skip, romp and roll, somersault or jump down the hall, or 'shake' while sitting in our places. The more variations the child can think of and manage the better. **no.25 instr.26**

H10

Theme Play

- While following each other in a line we repeat the actions that accompany the song. When sitting or lying down we stretch and bend our arms and legs and think of suitable sounds.

- Coloured pipe-cleaners can be left straight or bent to make figures. Use dough or clay to make straight rolls, count them and then join them together to make some meandering figures or suns.

- Contrasts: we play with hard and soft materials, thick and thin, big and small; we make something turn quickly or slowly.

- As we will be expressing emotions we could also think of games with 'frightened' and 'sad' feelings.

Write Dancing

Experiencing variations and recognising which movement goes with the music is fun and can be tried out either in movements, on the board or on paper. Always allow the children to think of sounds or expressive movements themselves, which will reinforce their personality. We will project these movements and noises on the writing surface. It will enable us to 'see' and 'hear' our feelings. The music will complement them in a pleasant way. Eye/hand/ear co-ordination is now well on its way.

H10

Expressions on the Writing Surface

Basic movement: alternation of straight and round lines, heavy and gentle pressure

It stands to reason that expressions on the writing surface during the 'straight' song will be represented as lines and that the 'krongelidong' song will present round lines and/or loops. Straight lines present assertive and confirmative feelings, while rounded lines give feelings of adjustment, collaboration and general relaxation and ease.

The lines could go in any direction while they are scrimbling and the children can let off steam and pretend to be cross. There are scrimbles consisting of upright movements and scrimbles consisting of flat movements, which will make a beautiful cross when combined. Please make them repeat the lines in the air to feel the difference, very big ones and tiny ones. The round movements may change spontaneously into loops or circling. Let the children find out for themselves if it makes them feel happy. We are trying out heavy and gentle pressure, also by finger dancing on each other's backs to really feel the difference.

Scrimbling: Writing Movements

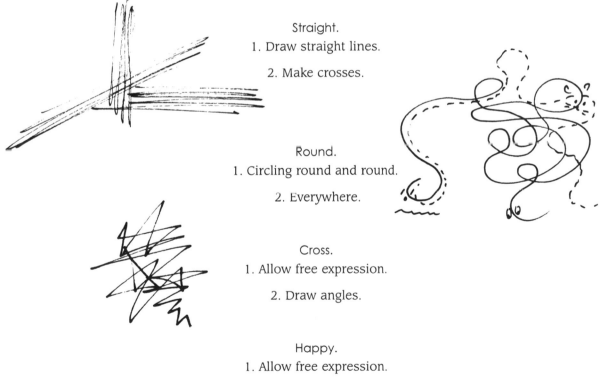

Straight.
1. Draw straight lines.

2. Make crosses.

Round.
1. Circling round and round.

2. Everywhere.

Cross.
1. Allow free expression.

2. Draw angles.

Happy.
1. Allow free expression.

2. Draw a figure and 'scrimble' freely round it.

Funfair Stories

F1

Watermill

Matching Theme Home:
Sandy Hill

Yoyo and Meema are going to the funfair with their Dad. They enter through a big gateway with lights. There is a lot of music and lots of noise and Meema skips with excitement while Yoyo strides ahead holding his Dad's hand.

'Look that's the shooting gallery,' says Dad, 'it might be too difficult for you, but we could go to the marquee where they throw balls.' They pass under the enormous roller-coaster. The roller-coaster cars make a screeching noise and Meema ducks down.

'Look, that's new,' says Yoyo and he points up at a very high post which shoots people up in a cabin, after which they drop down very, very, very quickly. The girls' long hair flies up in the air. They walk on a little and arrive at the tent with little watermills. It is more suitable for little children.

'Shall we stop here?' asks Meema and Yoyo and Daddy like it, too. There are five watermills in a row and there are three other children also choosing a watermill. The man gives them a big bucket of water and a small bucket or a watering can.

'You should take as much water as you can out of the big bucket with your little bucket and pour it into the trays, otherwise it will not turn,' says the man. Yoyo's mill is beginning to slow down and he adds more water. Meema has dropped her watering can, but it doesn't matter. The man has filled it up with water. The mill belonging to a girl called Emma is now turning very fast because she is pouring a lot of water into it. It is fun seeing all those turning mills. The children find all their water has gone and Yoyo and Meema return to their Dad.

Water from my bucket,
Water pouring fast,
Water from my bucket,
Water pouring fast,
The little mill is turning,
Turning... (8x)
Or else it doesn't work. (4x)

F1

Movements

Words	Movements
Water in my tumbler, Water pouring fast, Water in my tumbler, Water pouring fast,	Make pouring or watering movements.
The little mill is turning, Turning... (8x)	Turn wrists and arms round each other or turn around yourself.
And else it doesn't work. (4x)	Turn wrists and palms up or let yourself fall down on the floor or simply shake your head.
Water from my bucket,	Pretend you are pouring water from a bucket or watering can.
Water pouring fast,	Make pouring or watering movements.
Water from my bucket,	Pretend you are pouring water from a bucket or watering can.
Water pouring fast,	Make pouring or watering movements.
The little mill is turning, Turning... (8x)	Turn wrists round each other or turn around in your place.
And else it doesn't work. (4x)	Turn palms up or let yourself fall down.

78

F1

Theme Play

- Play with buckets, trays, beakers and coloured water thickened with glue. Make a mark on a piece of plastic and arrange for the 'mark train' to come along (see The Toy Train). It is possible to replace thickened water with sand, beads, marbles and so on.

- Cover bowls with paper-mache; dry and paint them. These bowls are hollow. Bigger plastic bowls can be used for hats; they are round.

- Fill a strong freezer bag with water and tie it. Cut a tiny point off and put it in a bucket after use. We scrimble on a big plastic sheet and with the small jet of water we try to make more lines. Next dry everything with your hands or cloths. You could replace water with fine sand from the pet shop.

- Invent games that combine hiding and water. Place a little object in a big bucket and pour a little black coloured water over it. The object has disappeared. If we continue to pour clear water over it the object will reappear.

Scrimbling: Writing Movements

Basic movement: rocking movements from side to side

Water from my bucket, (2nd verse)
Water pouring fast,
1. We make rocking movements from side to side.

2. Waves and drops.

The little mill is turning... (8x)
1. Turning in a circle.

2. Turning standing up.

And else it doesn't work. (4x)
Turn wrists up still holding the pieces of chalk in your hands.

F2

My Dinky Car

Matching Theme Home:
Kringeli-krangeli

Yoyo has thrown many balls in the marquee. He found it very difficult. Two out of ten balls passed through the hole, which was very good. Meema threw tins, but she didn't hit any and started to cry. Nevertheless both of them were allowed to choose a small prize. Yoyo chose a green lollypop and Meema a red one. They walk on very slowly and stop to look here and there.

'Look those are dinky dodgem cars,' says Dad. There are six of them and Yoyo gets in a blue one and Meema in a green one. They look like shoes and have cute faces. They both pop a coin in the slot and the cars start off. All you have to do is steer – how exciting.

'Mind your steering Meema,' says Dad, because Meema looks in all directions except straight ahead. Yoyo is quite good at it and has passed his Dad three times. He is really proud and imagines he is a lorry driver. Suddenly all the cars stop.

'Can we have another go?' asks Yoyo and they are given another coin to put in the slot.

'I am going to overtake you,' shouts Yoyo, 'but Meema doesn't mind, she is pretending her white car is a brand new trainer.

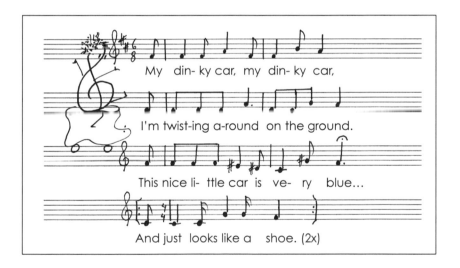

My din- ky car, my din- ky car,

I'm twist-ing a-round on the ground.

This nice li- ttle car is ve- ry blue...

And just looks like a shoe. (2x)

2nd verse	3rd verse
My dinky car, my dinky car,	My dinky car, my dinky car,
I'm twisting around on the ground.	I'm twisting around on the ground.
This nice little car is very black...	This nice little car is very white...
It's racing down the track. (2x)	And look I'm sitting tight. (4x)

F2

Movements

Words	Movements
My dinky car, my dinky car, I'm twisting around on the ground.	Steering movements. Swing both hands on one side of the body and squat down.
This nice little car is very blue...	Point at your nose (maybe the children can find something blue in their own clothes or somebody else's).
And just looks like a shoe. (2x)	Point at your shoe.
My dinky car, my dinky car, I'm twisting around on the ground.	Steering movements.
This nice little car is very black...	Point at something black.
It's racing down the track. (2x)	Run away quickly. Sitting down: intensive 'steering'.
My dinky car, my dinky car, I'm twisting around on the ground.	Steering movements.
This nice little car is very white...	Point at your teeth or something white.
And look I'm sitting tight. (4x)	Sit down in a position you like and don't move. The teacher walks round.

Note: All movements can also be performed sitting on the floor or on a stool.

82

F2

Theme Play

- 'Drive' a little car along a wriggly road drawn in chalk. We experience changes of direction, alone or together, we meet each other, avoid each other, follow each other, bump into each other, speed up, slow down and so on.

- In the sand you can make imprints of a variety of toy cars or other vehicles.

- We can also sing other transport songs, such as, 'The Wheels on the Bus'.

- Run a car along your own body or somebody else's: fast, slow, with more or less pressure. One child is lying on his tummy on the floor. Another child or teacher makes the vehicle jump like a flea or fly through the air like a fly and then it makes a surprise landing on a leg or on an upper arm... Sounds, anticipation and sudden surprises enhance excitement and tension.

Scrimbling: Writing Movements

Basic movement: twisting around with and without loops

My dinky car, my dinky car,
I'm twisting around on the ground.
'Drive' two pieces of blue chalk along the writing surface
(colour shaving foam blue with a drop of paint).

This nice little car is very blue...
And just looks like a shoe. (2x)
1. Make a 'scrimble track'; the chalk represents a car. Make noises.

2. 'Scrimble' a shoe.

2nd verse

My dinky car, my dinky car,
I'm twisting around on the ground.
'Drive' two black or dark pieces or chalk
(put a drop of dark paint in shaving cream).

This nice little car is very black...
It's racing down the track. (2x)
'Drive fast' along the writing surface.

3rd verse

My dinky car, my dinky car,
I'm twisting around on the ground.
'Finger-driving' = without pieces of chalk
or writing materials.

This nice little car is very white...
And look I'm sitting tight. (4x)
Sit still in a position you like.

F3

Merry-go-round

Matching Theme Home:
Pat-a-cake

Isn't it a beautiful old-fashioned merry-go-round at the funfair? The man looking after the merry-go-round proudly tells them that his grandpa bought it and that it is one hundred years old today. That is why everybody is presented with a small ice cream before getting on. There is a long staircase to the merry-go-round and you have to go up at least six steps. Yoyo chooses to sit on the elephant. Meema is sitting on a horse and the girl called Emma is back again. She is sitting on a giraffe that can bend its knees when the merry-go-round begins to turn. Next it goes up and down. Yoyo and Meema are sitting so high up that they can see the beach and the sea in the distance.

'Dad, our sand hill is still there,' shouts Yoyo.

'Hurray, the sea hasn't washed it away yet,' exclaims Meema. The merry-go-round has begun to turn.

Meema sings the song her teacher has taught her, 'Hold horsy tight, my horse has had a fright…'

'Tootah toot toot,' says Yoyo's elephant when he pushes a button behind the elephant's ear. But the giraffe doesn't say anything, it only bends its knees and leaves Emma's long hair waving in the wind. It is beginning to go dark, but they don't have to go home yet.

Hold horsy tight, my horse has had a fright. (2x)

Turn me round and round once more

And put me on the floor.

2nd verse

Tootah toot toot,
This really is a hoot.
Tootah toot toot,
This really is a hoot.
My arm is straight, my arm is bent
And round the bend we went.

3rd verse

Hip, hip, hooray,
I see my hill of sand
Hip, hip, hooray,
I see my hill of sand.
Wash it up ashore big sea,
But leave my hill to me.

F3

Movements

Words	Movements
Hold horsy tight, My horse has had a fright. Hold horsy tight, My horse has had a fright.	Alone: 'galloping' or jumping movements. Two by two: jump together, grab each other's hands.
Turn me round and round once more,	Alone: revolving movements with wrists or entire body. Two by two: hold tightly on to each other and spin around.
And put me on the floor.	Alone: sit down and/or make downward movements with arms. Two by two: sit on the floor opposite each other.
Tootah toot toot, This really is a hoot. Tootah toot toot, This really is a hoot.	Alone: 'blowing' movements with hands touching, mouth and arms stretched. Two by two: blow towards each other. Alone: continue 'blowing'. Two by two: grab each other's hands and move arms up and down.
My arm is straight, my arm is bent	Alone: stretch out one arm. Two by two: stretch arms and move away from each other. Alone: bend arm. Two by two: bend arms and get closer.
And round the bend we went.	Alone: spin around on your spot. Two by two: hold hands and turn arms round together.
Hip, hip, hooray, I see my hill of sand. Hip, hip, hooray, I see my hill of sand.	Alone: both arms raised up high. Two by two: while holding on to each other raise arms. Place one hand above the eyes (alone or together) Repeat.
Wash it up ashore big sea, But leave my hill to me.	Wave movements (alone or together). Shake head and continue making 'waves' (alone or together).

F3

Theme Play

- We walk round a hoop on the floor to the rhythm of the music and when the music is set to pause we stop a moment. Alternatively scatter some sponges round the hall and when the music stops all the children try and find a sponge.

- We have put five or seven hoops in the classroom and in the middle we see the merry-go-round man. He takes tickets or hands out ice creams. Any child in another hoop can imagine which animal or vehicle they represent.

- The teacher takes some chalk and draws an enormous circle on the floor helped by the children. Tie a piece of chalk to a piece of string of about a metre and tie a loop at the other end. One child holds the end with the loop and the teacher turns round with the chalk like a compass. The child has been closed in and has now become a merry-go-round herself.

- The older children can use the string to play Hold Horsy Tight.

Scrimbling: Writing Movements

Basic movement: revolving circular movements

Hold horsy tight,
My horse has had a fright. 2x
1. Turning round

2. Draw dots or dashes in one spot.

Turn me round and round once more,
1. Turning round (with pieces of chalk) above the writing surface.

2. Allow wrists to turn.

And put me on the floor.
1. Draw lines from side to side.
2. Draw dashes downward.

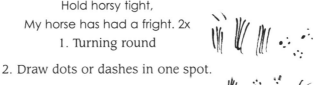

2nd verse	3rd verse
Toota toot toot, This really is a hoot. Draw long sweeping lines with arms ending up in the air.	Hip, hip, hooray, I see my hill of sand. Sweeping lines or dots.
My arm is straight, my arm is bent And round the bend we went. Stretch arm and bend it with chalk up in the air.	Wash it up ashore big sea, But leave my hill to me. Draw lines from side to side and simultaneously shake your head.

F4

The Procession

Matching Theme Home:
The Staircase

They can hear music in the distance.

'It's the brass band,' says Dad. 'Let's stand next to the cake stall and we will see them pass by.'

Isn't it exciting, what will the musicians' costumes be like? thinks Meema. More people join her and they all wait for the band to pass by.

Beat the drum! Beat the drum. Beat the big big drum. Everybody can hear it clearly.

Tootatoot-toot, hear the trumpet hoot. Meema is clinging onto her Dad because she is a little afraid. The music is getting louder. They are coming round the corner. Meema can see the girls wearing short green skirts. Holding her father's hand tightly she hops and skips to the music in her place. She is no longer tired, in fact she is feeling quite elated. The boys are wearing long trousers with yellow stripes down the sides.

'Can we walk along?' Yoyo asks, and he, too, is holding Dad's hand tightly. The three of them are marching to the rhythm.

The big drum is still beating loudly. And the trumpet is still hooting… toota toot-toot.

The procession proceeds under the big gateway of the funfair and Yoyo and Meema wave to the people in the procession.

'Bye, very big drum,' says Yoyo.

'Bye, tootatoot-toot,' shouts Meema.

Beat the drum, Beat the drum, Beat the big big drum.

Boys and girls come out to play, (2x)

Girls and lads play on the way. (2x)

Beat the drum, Beat the drum, Come and follow the drum.

2nd verse

Tootatoot-toot
Tootatoot-toot
Hear my trumpet hoot.

Beat the drum
Beat the drum
The sound of the very big drum.
Meema hops hippety hop
Yoyo slides steppety step
Meema hops hippety hop
Yoyo slides steppety step.
Beat the drum
Beat the drum
Come and follow the drum.
Beat the drum
Beat the drum
Come and follow the drum.

STOCKTON RIVERSIDE COLLEGE
Harvard Avenue, Thornaby, Stockton-on-Tees. TS17 6FB
OFFICIAL STAMP

F4

Movements

Words	Movements
Beat the drum, Beat the drum, Beat the big big drum. Beat the drum, Beat the drum, Beat the big big drum.	We pretend beating a big drum.
Boys and girls come out to play, Girls and lads play on the way. Boys and girls come out to play, Girls and lads play on the way.	Skirts: 'throw-away' movements from the hips. Trousers: slide hands slowly down legs, from the hips down past the knees.
Beat the drum, Beat the drum,	Beat the drum.
Come and follow the drum.	Hold each other's hands.
Beat the drum, Beat the drum, Come and follow the drum.	Repeat.
Tootatoot-tool, Tootatoot-toot, Hear my trumpet hoot.	Hold one hand near to your mouth, bend the other arm and stretch.
Beat the drum, Beat the drum, The sound of the very big drum.	Beat the drum.
Meema hops hippety hop, Yoyo slides steppety step. Meema hops hippety hop, Yoyo slides steppety step.	Hippety hop: jump up and down or sit and bob upper body up and down. Steppety step: take big, long steps (even when sitting down).
Beat the drum, Beat the drum,	Beat the drum
Come and follow the drum.	Hold each other's hands.
Beat the drum, Beat the drum, Come and follow the drum.	Repeat.

F4

Theme Play

- The teacher beats the drum in a marching rhythm and the children walk according to the beat. Alternate slow and quick drum beats. We take big steps on the slow beats and can pretend we are going upstairs.

- Let the children improvise and beat all kinds of things. The teacher has a little bell, a horn or some other kind of instrument. All the children are drumming and when the teacher gives them a sign they stop, or continue.

- Let the boys and girls dance round the room and play the song, 'I am so very happy'. Next ask them to walk around pretending to be cross. Boys and girls change expressions in turn.

- We can experiment with line formations: Follow each other in a line, and when the teacher gives a sign the one at the front walks to the back * or we walk in pairs, make a wriggly track, walk in a circle and so on.

- Repeat games with round and straight movements.

Scrimbling: Writing Movements

Basic movement: lines and dashes

Beat the drum,
Beat the drum,
Beat the big big drum. 2x

Draw dots and dashes with both hands to the rhythm of the music and of course with your own sounds, words and noises.

Boys and girls come out to play,
1. Draw sweeping lines to the left and right sides of the paper.

2. Speckle.

Girls and lads play on the way.
1. Draw lines downward.

2. Retrace with lots of colours.

2nd verse	3rd verse
Beat the drum,	Tootatoot-toot,
Beat the drum,	Tootatoot-toot,
Come and follow the drum.	Hear my trumpet hoot.
Scrimble and stamp your feet simultaneously.	Draw slanting lines from side to side and upwards.

Meema hops hippety hop,
Small fast specks.
Yoyo slides steppety step,
Big, long lines.

F5

Air Train

Matching Theme Home:

The Toy Train

'Toot toot!' says the funfair train. It is travelling along very high tracks in the air and has a cute face. When it travels its eyes open and shut. They are its lights. Yoyo tries to copy the movement with his eyes, but it isn't easy at all. There are so many wheels that it looks like a thousand.

'Just get in and then we will travel high up through the air and it doesn't cost anything at all,' says the air train conductor.

The three of them climb up another very long staircase with as many as ten steps. Meema's legs feel a little tired, but fortunately they are almost there. They get in and the guard closes all the doors firmly with a key.

'Right, now nobody can fall out,' says Dad. They can clearly see the sea and the beach. Yoyo and Meema's sand hill is far too far away, but they can see lots of windsurfers and kite surfers. One of the surfers takes an enormous leap up in the air.

'Did you see that Meema?' Yoyo gives her a nudge, but Meema was looking in the opposite direction. She saw a… Yes, what did she see? The air train is slowing down now.

'Toooot, toooot!' says the whistle and the train switches its headlight-eyes on and off.

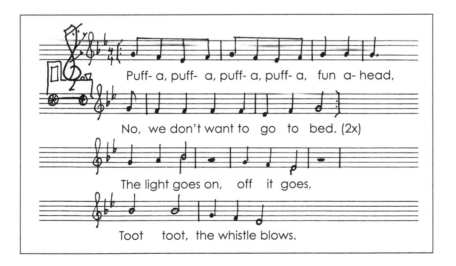

Puffa, puffa, puffa, puffa, fun ahead,
No, we don't want to go to bed.
Puffa, puffa, puffa, puffa, fun ahead,
No, we don't want to go to bed.
Open the door, shut the door,
My train rolls along the floor.

F5

Movements

Words	Movements
Puffa, puffa, puffa, puffa, fun ahead,	Make train movements with arms held tightly against the body.
No, we don't want to go to bed.	Slowly shake your head.
The light goes on,	Open eyes wide and/or stretch fingers wide.
Off it goes,	Close eyes and/or clench fingers into fists.
Toot toot, the whistle blows.	Pretend you are pulling the whistle.
Puff,a puffa, puffa, puffa, fun ahead,	Train movements.
No, we don't want to go to bed.	Shake your head.
Open the door,	Open door by hand.
Shut the door,	Shut door again.
My train rolls along the floor.	Roll along the floor.

F5

Theme Play

- We will do the same movements and express ourselves in the same way as we did with The Toy Train. What kind of sound does an air train make?

- The marks we made in the field of marks in The Toy Train theme, using confetti and snippets of paper or sand (outside), could represent clouds.

- Maybe the teacher knows some reading books about other vehicles that travel through the air, otherwise we will imagine some ourselves. What else can travel through the air? We continually allow our arms and wrists to turn along.

- If there is a long PE bench available the children could alternate riding on it on the floor and 'in the air', once again forwards and backwards.

- We repeat the exercise with legs open and shut. Next we add the 'downward dive' and dive on to the floor with our heads reaching forward right down to the floor.

- We place objects on the floor in a line and walk in and out of them in loops.

Scrimbling: Writing Movements

Basic movement: loops in a tangle or loops upward and downward

Puffa, puffa, puffa, puffa, fun ahead,
Draw loops over the entire writing area or make your own movements.

No, we don't want to go to bed.
Continue drawing loops, meanwhile shaking your head.

The light goes on, off it goes,
1. Don't move the pieces of chalk for a moment and open and close your eyes.

2. Circle round and round and draw cross bars through them.

Toot toot, the whistle blows.
1. Draw long lines from side to side.

2. Draw lines downward.

2nd verse

Open the door, shut the door,

1. Practise slowly using your voice: both hands draw lines away from the body (open) and back again towards the body (closed).

2. Repeat this many times, before you play the music.

My train rolls along the floor.

1. The child or teacher draws a face on the train, which is then consolidated by scrimbling movements.

2. Draw a number of faces.

Tree & Fairy Lights   Matching Theme Home:

Tickle Tree

It is growing dark and many of the lights at the funfair are lit. The trees are also lit. One tree has very many little lights: red, blue, green and white. They are flashing on and off. Meema would like to touch all those lights but they are too high up. The lights are flashing on and off, clip, clop. Yoyo closes one of his eyes so that he can have a better view of that one little red light and he pretends he can reach it.

Snatch, snatch, snatch is the movement he makes with his hands.

'Tomorrow I am going to draw a tree with lots of coloured specks in it,' he tells his Dad.

'Are you also planning to draw the big drum in the procession?' asks Dad, but Yoyo doesn't know yet. Those dotted lights are much easier. Now he can see a nice lady next to the tree who is also inspecting the lights.

'If you come and stand here, a bit further away from the noise, you can hear the song coming from the tree,' says the lady. The three of them follow the dear old lady.

Now they can hear the tree sing: All the little lights in the tree, I see you and you see me. It makes Yoyo and Meema laugh and Dad lifts them up high in turn, but the lights are still too far away.

'Thank you,' says Dad to the lady. Yoyo will now be able to sing this song tomorrow when he draws the dotted lights in his tree.

'I can also draw a big forest,' says Yoyo to the old lady and she gives him a kind smile and walks on.

All the little lights in the tree-ee,
I see you and you see me-e.
Cli- pper, cli- pper, cli- pper, clip, clop clop.

Red and blue and green and whi-ite,
All the little lights are so bri-ight.
Clipper, clipper, clipper, clip,
Clop clop.

F6

Movements

Words	Movements
All the little lights in the tree-ee, I see you and you see me-e.	Stretch arms and try and grab the 'lights' with thumb and fingers. Try to repeat this movement only using thumb and index, and thumb and middle finger.
Clipper, clipper, clipper, clip,	'Shake'.
Clop, clop.	Make strong fists.
Red and blue and green and whi-ite,	Grab 'lights' between thumb and fingers and possibly make little jumps.
All the little lights are so bri-ight.	Sit down on the floor or lower arms from high to low while sitting down.
Clipper, clipper, clipper, clip,	Snatching or shaking movements.
Clop clop.	Make strong fists.

F6

Theme Play

- Tap your own body or somebody else's gently with your fingertips. That is the way to express the flashing lights.

- Move hands and fingers around in shaving foam and scrimble. Use a pipette to add coloured drops. They can represent lights that slowly switch on and off.

- We can make a festive tree by sticking confetti, snippets of paper or cloth, rice, cotton wool balls to your 'scrimble tree'.

Scrimbling: Writing Movements

Basic movement: lines and specks

All the little lights in the tree,
1. Dashes and specks everywhere.

2. In a small constricted area.

I see you and you see me.
1. Add new specks on top of the previous ones

2. Draw small 'v' shapes.

Clipper, clipper, clipper, clip,
Clop clop.
1. Big or small dashes from side to side over the specks.

2. Draw cherries or apples and repeat the dashes.

2nd verse

Red and blue and green and white,
1. While standing we dot red and blue specks.

2. 'Green' and 'white' ones we will only do with our fingers.

All the little lights are so bright.
Children sit down on their chairs and continue speckling.

Clipper, clipper, clipper, clipper, clip,
Clop clop.
1. Quick or slow dashes or specks.

2. The teacher indicates the tempo and turns it into a game.

F7

Big Water Shute

Matching Theme Home:
Little Water Shute

It is almost completely dark at the funfair and it still feels quite warm. Yoyo and Meema have had two ice creams and a can of pop and they are still feeling hot. They are wandering round and think they have seen everything at the Funfair. But then…

'Look there's a water shute,' shouts Yoyo and runs on ahead. There are little boats which can take three people. Each boat looks like a fish. There is a small lake at the bottom where the boat can continue to wobble on the little waves for quite a while. Yoyo, Meema and Dad get into the blue dolphin. Right in front of them there is a little yellow boat with the face of a shark. It looks very angry and has a lot of big white teeth. A mother with two heavy boys gets into the shark boat. Oh, how it wobbles. The mother gets a shock, but laughs nevertheless.

The boats are pulled up by a chain, which is very exciting. Yoyo and Meema look in all directions and can see all kinds of things, the marquee with the balls, the cake stall, the merry-go-round, the dinky cars and the sea and the beach.

'Hold on tight, we have almost reached the top,' says Dad. The boat stops. The shark boat with the mother and two little boys has also stopped.

'I find this very scary,' they hear the mother call out.

'I will hold on to you, Mum,' says the biggest boy. He might be nine years old and he looks very strong. And then the shark boat swoops down at high speed with the mother and two boys. They hear the mother screaming at the top of her voice and they see that they have reached the bottom.

'Splash, splaaaaash,' says the water. Now it is Yoyo's and Meema's turn.

'Wow,' cries Yoyo, 'it is going terribly fast.' Meema keeps her eyes tightly shut.

'Splash, splosh, woosh,' says the water. They, too, went down very fast and the three of them are soaking wet.

'Great, that is just what we needed,' says Dad. They decide to go down again but this time they have to queue in a long line because many people have joined feeling hot and wanting to cool down in the boats on the water shute.

Rick- e- ty crick- e- ty boat green and blue,

I'd like to go for a row with you.

Spatter and splatter I'm not ready yet,

Look the boat made me terribly wet.

Dippety doppety dippety day,
Oh, there's so much fun today.
Move along and stand in a line,
Hurray it's now my second time.

F7

Movements

Words	Movements
Rickety crickety boat green and blue,	Arms and body make rolling movements.
I'd like to go for a row with you.	Point at each other.
Spatter and splatter I'm not ready yet,	Shaking movements.
Look the boat made me terribly wet.	Wrists and palms turn upwards. Give wrists a simultaneous powerful shake.
Dippety doppety dippety day,	Arms and body make rolling movements.
Oh, there's so much fun today.	Put hands against cheeks and move head from side to side with a smiling face.
Move along	Pushing movements with one or two hands.
and stand in a line,	Two hands make calm downward movements.
Hurray it's now my second time.	Arms stretched up in the air.

Theme Play

- Think of different ways to make a (wavy) water shute, for example, sticking empty packets of fruit juice together, fixing them on a raised platform where they can empty themselves into a tub. Make a thin wallpaper paste, put it in a beaker with acorns, chestnuts or other items and let it slide down.

- Have any of the children been down the big slide with their father, mother, brother or sister, and what did it feel like? What happens to the water when you crash down the slide with a big splash?

- We will fold boats out of paper and let them sail.

- A big sheet in the centre. Each child walks round the room to the music with their cuddlies. The cuddly toys could also make rolling movements to the music. When the music stops everybody places their cuddlies on the sheet. They are a little tired and we tuck them in to go to sleep.

- Put a bit of bath foam (preferably blue) on a big sheet of plastic. We are washing the cuddlies! Next we dry them with cloths and sponges.

Scrimbling: Writing Movements

Basic movement: swaying movements

Rickety crickety boat green and blue,
I'd like to go for a row with you.
1. Lines from side to side.

2. We will stick circles on paper so that we can draw waves round them. Slowly pronounce 'water' sounds (dippety, doppety) and then accompany by music.

Spatter and splatter I'm not ready yet,
Look the boat made me terribly wet.

1. Speckle the paper all over, for instance, using a toothbrush making waves and splashes.

2. When the surface is dry make new waves round the spots or twist around or draw loops, using different colours.

2nd verse

Dippety doppety dippety day,
Oh there's so much fun today.
Stripy or rolling movements from side to side.

Move along and stand in a line,
Hurray it's now my second time.
1. Dotting or drawing lines.

2. Scrimble figures and draw them.

F8

The Gateway

Yoyo begins to yawn with his mouth wide open, it's ten o'clock in the evening. Yoyo and Meema have never before gone to bed at that time, but it is holiday time so they don't have to get up early tomorrow morning to go to school. Meema asks if Dad will carry her, but Dad is tired, too, and therefore they decide to go home. Mum had already rung Dad's mobile because she was getting rather worried. Yoyo wanted to tell her everything immediately, but Mum replied that she was quite happy to wait until they got home. They saunter towards the exit.

'Can we have another bag of crisps?' asks Meema, but Dad says it will only make them thirsty and they might find something nice to eat in the car. The gateway at the exit is very big and lit up in beautiful rainbow colours. It looks like a real rainbow. Meema waves her arms from side to side pretending she is a big rainbow herself. Yoyo and Dad had walked on.

'Come on Meema, we really must go now,' says Dad. Meema remembers that Yoyo will want to draw a tree with lights in it. And I will draw a big rainbow, thinks Meema and she hops and skips to catch up with her Dad and brother.

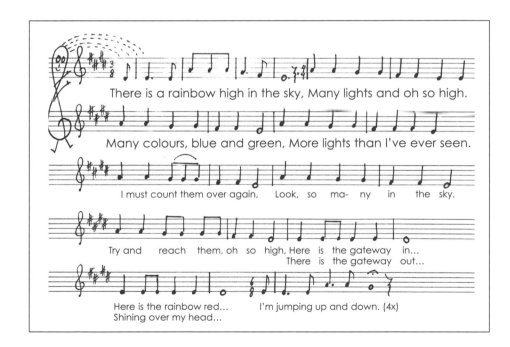

F8

Movements

Words	Movements
There is a rainbow high in the sky,	Make arches with arms fully stretched upward.
Many lights and oh so high.	Grabbing or thumb/index movements.
Many colours, blue and green,	Arched movements.
More lights than I've ever seen.	Grabbing or thumb/index movements.
I must count them over again,	Slowly shake your head.
Look, so many in the sky.*	Make pushing movement forward with both hands and fingers spread out, as if you are counting.
Try and reach them, oh so high,	Blow.
Here is the gateway in...	Each child points at their chest.
There is the gateway out...	Each child points into the distance.
Here is the rainbow red...	Move head and shoulders from side to side.
Shining over my head...	Make a big arch with both arms.
I'm jumping up and down.(4x)	Jump up and down in your place or alternate between allowing yourself to drop down and jump back up again.

F8

Theme Play

- If you have made a scrimbling den (see Materials for the Writing Surface), two children sitting on either side of the board, will be able to draw arches.

- The teacher will place two objects, for example, two drums, a meter apart. The other children will move from one drum to another in a big sweep.

Scrimbling: Writing Movements

Basic movement: arch shaped movements from side to side

There is a rainbow high in the sky,
Many lights and oh so high.
Many colour,s blue and green,
1. Draw lines from side to side.

2. We will stick a semi-circle on the paper, alternatively the teacher may draw one on the writing surface and we draw arches from side to side.

More lights than I've ever seen.
I must count them over again,
1. Speckle all over.

2. Shake your head and 'speckle-scrimble'.

Look, so many in the sky.
1. Specks along the rainbow.

2. Speckle to the rhythm.

Try and reach them, oh so high,
1. Lay down pieces of chalk and touch the specks with your fingers.

2. Make grabbing movement in the sky.

Here is the gateway in…
1. Point at a corner in the room.

2. Place the pieces of chalk on a corner of the writing surface.

There is the gateway out…
Choose another corner.

1. In the air.

2. On the writing surface.

Here is the rainbow red…
Draw a big arch on the writing surface.

Shining over my head…
Draw a new arch somewhere on the writing surface.

I'm jumping up and down. (4x)
Speckle all over and simultaneously make little skips in the air.

F9

Dear Sun, Dear Moon Matching Theme Home:
Little Sun

Dad starts the car engine. Vroom, is the sound the car makes with Yoyo and Meema in the back.

'Have you fastened your seat belts, because then we can go?' says Dad. Yoyo and Meema are so tired that they can hardly talk.

'Yes, we have,' Dad hears very faintly.

'Wasn't it a hot day,' says Dad after a while, 'and wasn't it great that the sun warmed up the funfair all day right into the evening?'

'Yes, because otherwise the water on the big water shute would have been far too cold,' says Yoyo.

'Do you think the sun will shine again tomorrow, Dad?' asks Meema.

'I think so,' says Dad, 'because the sun is always shining, but sometimes it doesn't break through the clouds and it is a grey day.'

'And this was a yellow day, wasn't it Dad,' says Meema and she hears Dad's little laugh.

'I suppose so, and what colour is it now Meema?' asks Dad. Meema looks up at the sky which hasn't yet turned completely dark and suddenly she sees the moon.

'Look the moon,' she cries excitedly, 'it is completely round tonight. Dad, would you mind stopping the car so that I can have a better view?' she asks.

Dad carefully slows down the car and parks the car at the side of the road. The three of them get out and have a look at the moon. The sky is almost completely dark with a little patch of blue and in the distance they can still see a couple of coloured strips of sun.

'Have people really set foot on the moon, Dad?' asks Yoyo.

'Yes,' says Dad, 'and I even saw the moon buggy on television when I was about your age.' Yoyo and Meema are too tired to ask any more questions.

'Thank you dear moon,' says Meema, ' for being so round tonight and having such a pretty face.'

'Come on,' says Dad, 'we must go home now otherwise Mum will be worried.' They get back into the car and Dad turns the ignition key.

'Vroom,' says the car and Yoyo and Meema fall asleep on their way home.

My dear sun, my dear moon,
My dear sun, my dear moon,
Going home this afternoon.
Thank you sun, thank you moon,
Thank you sun, thank you moon
I will be back, be back, be back,
Be back, be back very soon.

F9

Movements

Words	Movements
My dear sun, my dear moon, My dear sun, my dear moon,	Make two circles with both arms or wrists.
Flying home in a big balloon.	Turn your wrists upward and look sad.
Thank you sun, thank you moon, Thank you sun, thank you moon,	Blow hand kisses to the sun and the moon.
I will be back, be back, be back, Be back, be back very soon.	Run in all directions or from one corner to the next. Sitting down: stamp your feet on the floor.
My dear sun, my dear moon,	Make two circles.
My dear sun my dear moon,	Point at your chest.
Going home this afternoon.	Hand kisses.
Thank you sun, thank you moon,	Two circles.
Thank you sun, thank you moon,	Point at someone else.
I will be back, be back, be back, Be back, be back very soon.	Run or stamp your feet.

F9

Theme Play

- The same variations as in the Home theme Little Sun can also be applied here.

- Make a mobile with suns and moons. Ask the children to scrimble and fill a strong piece of paper with paint or wax crayons. Once the shapes have been cut out it is possible to draw faces on them.

- Making and scrimbling stars also belong to this theme. We can finger dance and 'draw' the rays of the sun or a star on a wet board out from the centre.

- Play with shaving foam.

Scrimbling: Writing Movements

Basic movement: circular movements

My dear sun, my dear moon,
My dear moon, my dear moon,

1. Circle round and round – draw a big circle or different circles with both hands.

2. Split the 'sun(s)' or 'moon(s)' in two halves.
Scrimble half moons over them.

Flying home in a big balloon.
Draw wriggly lines down or draw a big balloon with a path up to it in squiggly lines.

Thank you sun, thank you moon,
Thank you sun, thank you moon,
1. Clasp hands together.

2. Frame the writing surface by scrimbling straight lines on the left and right.

I will be back, be back, be back,
Be back, be back very soon.
Draw speckles towards the scrimbled suns and moons.

2nd verse

Thank you sun, thank you moon,
1. Point upwards.

2. Point at moon or sun drawings on the writing surface.

MORE WRITE DANCE TITLES

from Lucky Duck

Write Dance

A Progressive Music and Movement Programme for the Development of Pre-Writing and Writing Skills in Children

WITH AUDIO CD! 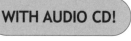 **WITH VIDEO**

Ragnhild Oussoren

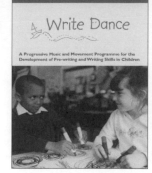

'The author of this book is a very experienced graphologist who has worked on the subject with children for many years. What she has produced is a highly practical resource for early years teachers' - *Special*

'The whole scheme is wonderfully inventive and gives a wealth of ideas to be developed and adapted to suit a particular group of children. It uses a wide range of movements with a greater variety of direction than many pre-writing schemes and encourages the children in their movements quickly as well as rhythmically, with confidence and enjoyment' - *Handwriting Today*

This innovative and exciting programme is widely used across Europe as a way of introducing handwriting using music, movement and exercise. It has been found especially helpful for children with special educational needs, from learning difficulties to dyspraxia.

Psychologists working with youngsters with learning difficulties developed the idea. It was thought that encouraging children to express themselves would empower them and raise their self-esteem. The experts soon noticed that it benefited children of all abilities, and once they started writing, letters were better formed and more legible.

The **Write Dance** programme is sold as a fully comprehensive package including: Instruction Book, CD music recording and training video. Items can also be bought separately. If you have already bought the pack items, you can purchase replacement items separately.

Contents

What is Write Dance? \ What is Writing Psychology? \ Teaching Writing in Sweden in the 1990s \ How is the Write Dance Programme Organised? \ At What Age Should Write Dance Be Introduced? \ Is the Write Dance Method Tied to any Prescribed Style? \ The Teaching Principles of the Write Dance \ The Rhythm of Handwriting \ Practical Explanation - Ideas and Tips \ Blindfolds \ The Writing Movement Test \ Learning to Write \ Write Dance Daily Practise \ The Write Dance Programme \ The Volcano \ A Walk in the Country, Krongelidong \ Circles and Eights \ Robot \ The Train \ The Growing Tree \ Silver Wings over the Sea \ Cats \ Mandala \ Carry On...with Write Dance \ Clowns and Shy Children \ Combining Music with Imaginative Drawings \ The Story that Connects all Themes \ Write Dance Folding Books \ Lectures and Inset Days

2000 • 81 pages
Video, paperback and audio CD (1-87394-203-6)
Paperback (1-4129-1243-1)
Audio CD (1-4129-1239-3)
Video (1-4129-1242-3)

More Write Dance

Extending the Development of Write Dance for Children Aged 4 to 8

WITH AUDIO CD! **WITH VIDEO**

Ragnhild Oussoren

Since the launch of **Write Dance** in UK Primary schools, five very successful years have passed and now teachers are asking, "What can we do next?"

More Write Dance provides even more resources and teaching materials on this lively, exciting and tremendously fun approach to developing pre-writing and writing skills. The theory and the philosophy are explained in much greater depth, and more music, instructions and illustrations are provided to guide and inform teachers and children on how to move and 'move-draw' to refine and to develop their movements and their drawings to achieve fluent letter strings, with ease and speed.

The **Write Dance** principles of raising children's awareness of their own emotions in order to be more confident to express themselves comfortably still apply. The book is suitable for those new to the approach as well as those already familiar with it.

Contents

THE WRITE DANCE PHILOSOPHY \ Write Drawing and Writing in Your Own Swing and Style \ WRITE DRAWING \ Exercises as a Preparation and Support of Writing \ Sensorial Motor and Breathing Exercises \ Playing With Cartoon-Animals \ LISTENING TO LETTERS \ Learning How to Write in the Write Dance Way: From Movements to Shapes in Your Own Personal Space \ Writing Sheets: Copy-Sheets for Write Movements \ Fantasy-Letters and Soundwords \ SIX NEW MUSIC DRAWINGS \ Exercises for Gross Motor Skills and Fine Motor Skills \ Working On Wide Lines and in the Copybook

June 2006 • 96 pages
Paperback and audio CD (1-4129-1871-5)
Audio CD (1-4129-2170-8)
Video, paperback and audio CD (1-4129-2171-6)

www.PaulChapmanPublishing.co.uk

Paul Chapman Publishing
A SAGE Publications Company

Lucky Duck Publishing